*Abigail and Chloe Baldwin*

# THE BRAND
# POWER
# MANIFESTO

BRANDING BRILLIANCE FOR

FEMALE ENTREPRENEURS

*BIS Publishers*

BIS Publishers

Borneostraat 80-A
1094 CP Amsterdam
The Netherlands
T +31 (0)20 515 02 30
bis@bispublishers.com
www.bispublishers.com

ISBN 978 90 636 9702 0

*In memory of our Granddad,*
*who always adopted the "ready for anything" motto.*

# CONTENTS

# FOREWORD

*Sir John Sorrell &*
*Lady (Frances) Sorrell*

———————————

*Founders of the Sorrell Foundation and the National Saturday Club*

Creativity is an important part of Britain's identity as an innovative nation. Our creative industries are a success story economically and socially, making our reputation for edgy brilliance and business success.

The country needs more and more vibrant young entrepreneurs to bring fresh ideas, imagination and drive to grow our creative sector and build local and international commercial partnerships. One of the exciting things for us is to see young people in the National Saturday Club, which is for 13-16-year-olds, develop their talents and seize the opportunities which unfold on their learning journeys.

We first met Chloe and Abigail in 2010 when the Sorrell Foundation was prototyping the National Saturday Club and they joined the Club in Leeds. They progressed on to University and then worked incredibly hard to create and build their business and its unique approach which people really like. We are impressed by the way they talk about partners rather than clients and it is easy to see why people want to work with them. As well as their skills in design and illustration they are well organised, think strategically and are full of ideas, positivity, resilience and sheer joy in creativity. They are the kind of partner in business everybody needs.

Chloe and Abigail are immensely courageous, not just in taking the risks that are necessary if you are to grow and succeed but also by giving time to encourage others to believe in themselves.

They are great role models and we are proud to know them.

 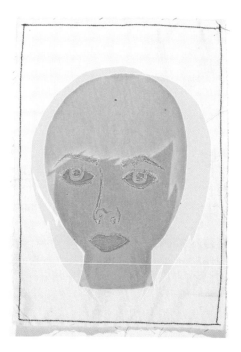

^ *We created these screen printed portraits during our time on the National Saturday Club's programme. The prints were exhibited at Somerset House, London.*

> *Our "twinship". We have always loved being creative together, so it seemed only natural that we would work in partnership. We can't get away from each other!*

A comic illustration by Abigail and Chloe for the National Saturday Club's annual newspaper (2021). It shares the story of how the Club provided a launch pad.

# Chapter 1

# INTRODUCTION

*The Journey Calls*

---

## 1.1 WHAT IS THE BRAND POWER MANIFESTO?

When building a business, it can feel overwhelming when you think of the journey wholly. Branding can act as the compass to help you steer the ship and find confidence. Plus, it does not need to be a mammoth task. Instead take a step-by-step approach with The Brand Power Manifesto. This roadmap helps chart the course and keeps the wind in your sails. The book covers the following stages:

1. Use your peripheral vision: An insight into strategic brand analysis
2. Make it powerful: Find the core of your brand
3. Give the people what they want: Communicate your unique value proposition
4. Use your magic: Gain credibility and be taken seriously
5. Your network is your net worth: Nurture relationships and build community
6. Make it matter: Implement what you've learnt
7. You got to know when to hold 'em, know when to fold 'em: Track and pivot to stay relevant
8. Stay curious: Keep looking to the future

This modular system and empowering manifesto can help build a brand, one step at a time.

If you're interested in entrepreneurship, but feel the loom of imposter syndrome, we've written this manifesto for you.

After all, some people are natural-born entrepreneurs. They are born with an eye for opportunity, the gift of the gab, and steely determination. These admirable beings can sniff out a gap in the market, create solutions for their customers and run a business which doesn't run them. They've got an exit plan and they're on the road to success.

Then, some people are following the path that is placed before them with no real intention — then BAM — they have a business! Maybe they were whittling wood, teaching children to swim, or arranging floral displays, purely for joy. Then one day, their neighbour recognised their skill and agreed to an exchange. The exchange was successful, and they tell all their friends. Before you know it, the whittler is a sculptor and the swimmer is a coach.

Both groups are business people, however, we fall into the latter category.

## *1.2*   WHO ARE WE?

Our business, Buttercrumble, sprouted organically from a love of design and illustration. It's challenging to envisage a time before creativity took hold. We believe everyone is born with the ability to create and we summon its power in different ways. This is what sets humankind apart.

As teenagers, we began sharing our primitive, creative experiments online for feedback. We were independent, at first, working under two separate usernames: Abblecrumble and Butterscones. However, being twin sisters, we knew "two heads are better than one"! We merged our usernames to become the one we are today, Buttercrumble. Enabled by platforms such as DeviantArt and Fiverr, we began to share our work and secure regular commissions. Despite the fact we were both illustrating characterful portraits for people around the world, the monetisation didn't click. In our eyes, we were doing something for the joy of it, and the money was a bonus.

We discovered this joy much earlier in our life before we had access to the internet. It was a rainy day and so we were imprisoned in our classroom. To fight her itchy feet, Chloe started doodling and illustrated every member of the class in a humorous typology. Before long, the news of this epic doodle spread and everyone was asking to see the handiwork. Everyone wanted a piece of the action and — oh — the joy it brought. We had experienced the unifying power of creativity.

As children, we'd always be playing make-believe. Our favourite game involved an impressive collection of TY Beanie Babies. Each toy was assigned a character with its special role to play; it was essentially a soap opera within our bedroom! We used our toys to narrate stories by designing characters with real voices. Their voices were so developed that if we had friends around to play with, the Beanie Babies were off limits to our guests. After all, they'd never be able to catch up with each character's history and development! We loved exploring narratives through the toys. We developed these soap operas using illustration as we found it could be a powerful story-telling tool. When drawing, the only limit was our imagination.

Moreover, we realised creativity can serve a purpose. Our first request (or commission) came from our Mum following a calamity! She pushed her hand through the weak glass of our kitchen door — ouch! Thankfully, she was okay and briefed us to illustrate a series of pictures to conceal the empty pane. The illustrations, painted by our five-year-old selves, were far from mini Da Vinci's. However, they patched the hole and added visual and sentimental interest to the home. A win-win situation! Of course, our Mum was one happy customer and has been an ambassador for us ever since.

Meanwhile, our outside activities were always more perilous. Perhaps this explains the comfort we find in quiet indoor activities. Our large garden was home to a swing ball, a slide and our Super Soakers. Unfortunately, British weather is not always accommodating to these activities so we'd shelter by taking it in turns to lock each other in the "dungeon". This was effectively a cupboard underneath the garage.

We'd also foolishly swing on the driveway's chain fencing, Chloe would usually over-egg it and whack her little egghead on the hard pavement.

The worst event involved scooters and a trip to the hospital when Abigail broke her leg, aged six. Yes, it's no wonder we retreated to the warmth and comfort of indoors. Pass the crayons, please!

Forming our business has always felt like an organic process. When we reflect on our journey, we realise we've been subtly directed on this path by a squad of cheerleaders (especially in education). From our very first class at the age of four, we felt encouraged to participate in creative activities.

## ABIGAIL'S REFLECTION

❝ I've always known we'd do something creative as a living. Passion has changed our lives. We've loved nothing else quite so much and I'm not sure what would be a better fit. Alternatives feel unbearable. That's why we infuse as much love as we can into the brand. The brand is a vehicle that communicates our vision further than we can. You have to infuse your brand with the love for your organisation.

During this creative enlightenment, we were six years old and it was the turn of the 21st century. SunnyD was the must-have beverage, so we're looking back with orange-tinted glasses. It matches my memories, perfectly — bright and positive. It was a time when the world was freaking out about the infamous "Millennium Bug", reality TV was just beginning to boom with the likes of Big Brother, and gaming boomed with the launch of the PlayStation 2. Everything felt fun and exciting with the development of technology. I knew the world was changing and it all felt like a huge novelty to us. This powered our imagination.

Creativity gives people a voice and a tool for self-expression. That's why we're so enthusiastic to share this tool — to do good and make a difference in people's lives through their businesses. After all, being a business owner is tough! We know that a dash of creativity (and branding) can do a lot of the hard work for you.

The crinkle of paper, pencils rolling across the table and the discussion of ideas as they whoosh through our minds! We loved drawing together at our dining room table. It was an activity that we could truly collaborate on.

I believe everyone can be creative and it occurs naturally. With a spark of the imagination, you have an idea in mind and sometimes it's so fleeting, you quickly have to scribble it down! For us, it's a desperate feeling to translate the vision into a reality. In the beginning, it can be frustrating as you can't always achieve an exact realisation. It's the frustration that can drive you to keep trying, learning and improving. This is why we love to use this skill to help others, we can realise visions through illustration and design.

. . . . . . . . . . . . . . . . . . .

## CHLOE'S REFLECTION

❝ Our teacher briefed the class to produce an illustration of a sporting event so we feverishly grabbed the felt tips and got cracking! Abigail and I often sit together, heads positioned closely, avidly scribbling away. We both illustrated ourselves in running races with exaggerated gangly legs and arms, our ponytails stuck out in the breeze, and rosy red cheeks (the redness being the most accurate observation). I can remember these artworks being no Picasso's, nonetheless, our teacher was thrilled by the outcomes. She displayed the illustrations publicly — in the school hallway — on a presentation board. The artworks (along with a Christmas tree illustration I created) were showcased for many years.

We will never forget this initial praise and encouragement although it also sparks a few unwanted memories. Along with that praise came a firm telling off when I didn't colour in a bear sufficiently. This is always an upsetting thought as I genuinely believed I did my best… colouring-in sheets just don't hold the same level of excitement as drawing from scratch.

This formed a pattern throughout our schooling journey, even when we moved schools, creative cheerleaders followed us. In the Easter of 2003, we transferred to another primary school and I remember the anticipation which filled our tummies. I felt uncharacteristically confident on our first day, showing off to the other children, and grappling the social ladder. On our first day, we were ushered to the front of the assembly hall as the other children were arriving. We were introduced to our head teacher who asked us if we enjoyed art, we told him it was our favourite subject, and he expressed a shared passion for the subject.

Our love of art and design continued to be nurtured throughout our time at primary school where we attended a newly formed art club. The club was mainly attended by boys who enjoyed illustrating comic book characters and cars. But, we like to think we introduced a feminine touch to proceedings with our whimsical drawings. When I look back, I notice many children enjoy observation and realism. They want to recreate a dream car they've spotted in a magazine or cartoons they love to watch. That was a little boring to us, we fell in love with story-telling, the imagination, and producing something from our wildest fantasies. This often included chocolate, desserts, and all things sweet!

In 2013 we moved schools again. Despite being placed in a standard form group, we noticed our timetable didn't match up with our peers. We had been selected to participate in extra art classes, taking our art qualifications early. We wondered if this was a strike of luck or something devised by our tutors. It must have been a bit of both. We were lucky enough for the opportunity and our previous school recognised our enthusiasm. This must have been communicated to our new school. We were also able to access college early thanks to the support we received at secondary school. Our art teacher was a real cheerleader and we were lucky that she recognised our passion.

When we transitioned into our penultimate school year, we could specialise in subjects and earn the respective qualifications. Naturally, we both wanted to study art and design; it was a no-brainer and we happily submitted our forms. The weeks passed and we received notice of our timetables for next year.

Where was art? Why was I up for acting? What a nightmare… drama was one of my least favourite subjects due to a string of embarrassing and unfortunate incidents.

It was Autumn in 2004 and we were rehearsing for the school nativity. I was finally promoted from shepherd to angel, a more glamorous role, and I donned my wings. I took this role very seriously as I felt liberated from my tea towel headdress and enthusiastically flew around the stage. Suddenly, the teacher-turned-director turned scarlet. "What do you think you're doing?" She screamed. The commotion was a bit confusing. Had I missed something? She continued to yell and approached the stage when I realised she was addressing me. "Angels don't flap their wings!" She thought I was joking around! I had never been so humiliated… Maybe shepherding wasn't so bad?

Drama classes at secondary school got a whole lot worse as I was heckled off stage and the audience substituted rotten tomatoes for pencils and paper spit-balls. I didn't want to risk that embarrassment again and I thought it was all behind me.

I sheepishly addressed the deputy headteacher and co-ordinator who delivered a flat-out no. I couldn't change acting to art. Exasperated, I turned to my art teacher for help who marched me back to the deputy. I was studying art.

She bolstered our art skills and drove us to the sixth-form college every Friday afternoon to complete additional art lessons. She also enrolled us in the National Saturday Club where we continue to partner in a more professional capacity. We felt at an advantage for university and higher education.

We are campaigners and advocates for education as it's catapulted us to success. We're witnessing a recent focus on science, technology, engineering and mathematics within the school due to the industry opportunities. Schools are hard-pushed with limited resources so it's understandable that with this intense focus, something has got to give. Unfortunately, we've found these to be arts subjects.

. . . . . . . . . . . . . . . . . .

We are not alone in our quest, there is a need and want for more creative opportunities — especially for women. We once had the pleasure of meeting retail expert and agency owner, Mary Portas. She told us to use our special power to connect with others and we always keep that golden nugget in mind. Mary chatted about her book "Work Like a Woman" which we've had the pleasure of reading. The book's insights resonate with us as she describes our untapped potential (2018). There is limited support for female-led businesses from both consumers and the government. Perhaps many people see women in business as hobbyists or better-suited to low-pay pursuits like self-employed cleaners or carers. Self-employed women earn approximately half the weekly salary of a woman in full-time employment, according to Portas (2018).

Creativity is a trait which isn't always valued. Yes, you are seen as useful and resourceful, but it's not always reflected in your pay-cheque. Money talks in business and it is often those in finance or sales who see the best rewards. This attitude has to change. Creativity is fundamental to problem-solving. Creativity kick-starts innovation. Creativity challenges the norm.

## CHLOE IN PURSUIT OF CREATIVITY

❝ We were due to go to Hong Kong in December 2019 to attend Business of Design Week. This is a leading annual event on design, innovation and brands. The event schedule boasts inspiring conferences, creative exhibitions, and satellite and pop-up events. It's no wonder it attracts industry leaders from around the world. It's a key date for many business professionals, property developers, academia, construction, retail and heritage organisations.

However, with political and social unrest, it was a turbulent time for the region. Large-scale protests were broadcast on our news stations weekly and the decision was made to cancel Business of Design Week. This was a huge disappointment to us as we had spent hours preparing, we had travelled across the country to briefing meetings, we'd printed business cards, and we even arranged meetings in Hong Kong.

What were we going to do? This was a once-in-a-lifetime opportunity.

Abigail and I can be pretty risk-averse as entrepreneurs, but this was no time to pussyfoot around — we were super-pumped for our trip! Despite the cancellation and the Department for International Trade's decision, we proceeded with our trip. Sometimes you have to be fearless in the pursuit of creativity. We listened to the Government's advice about travel, took reasonable precautions, and joined expatriate groups for news updates. We had never travelled to Asia and it was the furthest we'd ever ventured, but we were prepared for the adventure.

A full day of travel was pursued. We arrived at Leeds train station at midday and travelled down to Kings Cross London. From there, we caught the tube and Heathrow Express, before catching the plane. We arrived in Hong Kong the following day (late afternoon) thousands of miles away from home. As a creative, even the most mundane can spark inspiration. I'm not sure how inspiring an airport is to most people, but it was eye-opening to us. The space was expansive, modern, and oh-so-spotless. Also, who else loves seeing what foreign edible goodies can be found in convenience stores?

Travel is an essential experience we should all have. St Augustine once said "the world is a book and those who do not travel, only read a page". It widens your perspective and gives you a more empathetic outlook on life. We drove into Hong Kong City, towards the hotel, with pure amazement. We couldn't believe the sight of towering skyscrapers, embellished with thousands of tiny lights, they emphasised the crowded living arrangements. Almost every window framed a resident's silhouette all metres apart. You realise the world is too big to comprehend and much bigger than your own. Did we think all of these people knew our story? Cared about the city we live in? Knew about Business of Design Week? No. Everyone's living out their own story, in their own world. Suddenly your problems aren't as big as you first thought.

Despite the jet lag, our first true experience of travel fatigue, our first few days in the city were jam-packed. Boy, are we creatures of habit! It was difficult to navigate the city when your body clock is off-kilter but it was worth it (Hong Kong Disneyland certainly helped).

We anticipated our first business meeting with excitement. We had an appointment to see a Hong Kong children's brand in Sheung Wan, slightly West of the main business district, on Hong Kong Island. It was a bustling place and we pounded the pavements in the warm December sunshine. We dashed up and down the irregular curbs, dodging queues out of the bakeries, workmen handling bamboo, and bumbling taxis. Where is it? Where is it? The narrow streets and tall buildings make it tricky to get your bearings but we arrived with plenty of time to explore.

Eventually, we decided we found the building which was 1980s style and unassuming. The narrow doorway led into a reception area guarded by a stout female security guard. We stood outside to partake in a chorus of;

"You first!"

"No, you!"

"No… what should we say?"

"What was their address again?"

Anyway, we got over our nerves and entered the building. We greeted the security guard who didn't speak any English, but we managed to ask for our meeting, and she kindly showed us to the lift. The lift ride was a nerve-racking experience, we couldn't see where we were headed, and we didn't know what to expect when the doors opened. To our surprise, the doors opened directly in front of the office we were attending. There was nowhere to hide now!

Our first meeting passed smoothly, we had a wonderful conversation and gained a better understanding of the industry. The company politely provided us with top tips for our trip and we stayed in touch when we returned. The three meetings which followed this observed a similar outcome. We found the people to be pleasant, encouraging, and extremely hospitable.

This was especially true when we were invited to attend the China Club for one meeting. The private member's club is on the thirteenth floor of The Old Bank of China building and the 1930s interior decor was provided by our hostess. The experience was wonderful and we spent hours in discussions over the most beautiful dim-sum we've ever eaten. We were grateful to our hostesses who were attentive, ready to talk business, and didn't let us pay a penny. What a super experience for a pair of small-town girls. We travelled across the world to have a business meeting, with a children's fashion brand, overlooking the city. Think big and then think bigger.

Our Hong Kong adventure taught us to be fearless in the pursuit of creativity. The blend of Western and Eastern design was a feast for our eyes. It confirmed our suspicions surrounding a heightened preference for illustration in Asia than in Western markets. We were also excited by the retail experience in Hong Kong which felt far more developed than our offering in the UK. They pay clear attention to their facilities and introduce special animations to entertain and reward shoppers. They're not building a 'high street', they're building a community. We, at Buttercrumble, are passionate about introducing a more holistic, experiential approach to service design.

It also taught us to be wary of the media. Yes, the protests are real and happening. There is reason and sense behind the unrest and we respect Hong Kong's need for freedom. They have worked hard to build a glowing and respected identity. However, the news broadcast a heightened snapshot of day-to-day life in Hong Kong. Only one day (in our ten-day trip) was disrupted by protests and the disruption caused no distress to us. There we were sharing our daily, delicious, egg-puff-waffle dessert when a friendly lady approached us. The Hongkonger tentatively asked if we were tourists and we nodded (mouths full of ice cream). The stranger advised us to return to our hotels as a protest was starting soon and pointed to a young man dressed in black with the synonymous black face mask. We returned to the hotel safely and enjoyed a takeaway. I suppose that's not newsworthy though?

. . . . . . . . . . . . . . . . . . .

We believe the pursuit of creativity and — not forgetting — innovation are persistent for business owners. Whether you're a start-up or a business mogul, you need to stay relevant to your audience. The pursuit will always be ongoing for us. For example, our first portfolio was "me, me, me" and it fell flat. Our initial brand was fairly naive and didn't communicate the benefits of working with us but we knew we wanted to help others through the power of good design! We want to share with you our own experience of finding our business feet, discovering our customers, and being brave enough to pivot.

Furthermore, we acknowledge in recent years we've seen an increase of women in creative industries and leadership roles, but we are still in the minority. The journey has been challenging. We are two young women in our 20s who grew up in a low socio-economic area with no business experience. Our story shares a down-to-earth, real perspective of starting a business (from scratch) with no frills, bells, whistles, or mummy or daddy's money.

We share our story alongside practical advice and plenty of prompts to help you, whether you're starting your business, or taking your branding to the next level with clarity and confidence. We'll cover analysis, your brand's core, your value proposition, business relationships, implementation and evaluation written in plain easy-to-read language. We are Yorkshire lasses, after all! We mean what we say and say what we mean.

Competition is hotter than ever — how can you cut through the noise? We've written this book to help you kick-start your brand. You can start your dream business, celebrate your magic and become the go-to destination for your customers. Believe us, this is totally within your reach, and you don't need a huge financial investment or a business degree.

There are no rules in business and every entrepreneur's story is different.

Yes, running a business doesn't need to be a slog.

Yes, you are in control.

Yes, you don't need to constantly prove yourself.

## *1.3*   WHAT IS BRANDING?

Branding is a collection of devices you use together to set an expectation for customers. The right branding can push customers to pick you over your competitors, so it's important to give it careful consideration.

Branding is becoming increasingly popular. The topic "branding agency" has quadrupled in interest from January 2004 to March 2020 (Google Trends, 2020). Why? In this crowded marketplace, organisations are taking bold steps in building a brand to cultivate loyalty. This has accelerated in recent years due to the growth of the internet and social media. This has become a catalyst for the formation of new independent businesses. Technology has helped remove barriers to entry and provided access to research and support, resulting in many fresh and innovative organisations.

When building your business or climbing the career ladder, a lack of confidence, funding, and experience can cause issues. This is where brilliant branding can boost the organisation's credibility, despite a lack of resources, heritage or equity. It's a case of "dress for the job you want, not the one you have". By evaluating a brand's style and substance (rather than just functionality) organisations can visualise and magnify their assets and values. Additionally, start-ups without a clear brand strategy leave themselves open to attacks. After all, it's difficult and ineffective to copy a personality. Consider enhancing your brand's personality to help you develop a powerful identity. It can greatly impact perceptions with a small amount of investment. It communicates your organisation's unique value proposition and offers you a competitive edge. This is the power of branding.

The way we see it, how we create and manage brands is changing. Models, structures and guidelines are becoming too restrictive. Organisations want to communicate in a more inclusive, holistic and flexible way as audiences are seeking more authentic lifestyle brands. As a result, we should see the brand as an "effect". If you take action to do the right things as opposed to crafting a complex strategy, growth will follow.

To encourage growth, start with your brand purpose, and ask yourself: "Why?" Why is your brand going to be useful in people's lives? You need to decide how you can make a change in your customers' lives. The purpose is often lost in people's need for positioning, we obsess over the market, and our competition. High-growth companies focus on purposeful actions to drive results — they don't sweat over what their neighbour is doing — they ask themselves: "Why"?

Furthermore, many start-ups get hung up on their brand name, logo, colour scheme and tagline independent of each other. They consider each of these elements separately without joined-up thinking, resulting in a new identity with no coherence or meaning. Take a 360° approach to branding and design from the outside-in. Brands are experiences that consumers shape for themselves. How would your customers like to interact with your brand? You should make it easy for your audience to select you as their "go-to" choice.

We appreciate and respect the importance of brand guidelines, but don't let them stunt your growth. Keep evaluating and experimenting with your branding to discover what generates the best results. Our future is constantly evolving and changing, and so are our customer's needs. Don't create boundaries which stop you from revolutionising and moving with the times.

We see ourselves as Brand Guardians and there are many dimensions to managing a brand. As Guardians, we must set a long-term strategy, define and maintain brand purpose, manage communication and evaluate the brand's performance.

A brand guidelines document is a great tool to manage your brand in a structured way. You can also manage your brand through your company-wide culture. This can then be controlled by the senior level or within smaller groups. Some businesses prefer to review their brand position and image yearly whilst others will continue to innovate and change.

Now, we're not the "Identity Police" who clamp down on marketing teams, we like to collaborate and cultivate the right brand image. We protect the integrity of a brand whilst leaving room for creativity. It's important to maintain a sense of cohesion to build familiarity with customers and employees; you don't need to stifle the business.

Creating a level of cohesion can be rather straightforward for small independent brands. Yet, some companies work with multiple brands (inside and outside their organisation). When an organisation expands in this way they form a brand architecture system. This is to ensure that the different segments can work collectively without confusing customers.

**Brand architecture models usually follow one of four formats:**

★ **Portfolio** — Brands with different offerings and maximum flexibility (the brands can be unrelated). This approach spreads the risk as you don't keep your eggs in one basket.
★ **Family** — Brands with different offerings under a strong ethos and personality. This allows the organisation to cross-sell.
★ **Endorsed** — This approach is similar to a portfolio but each brand must share a common focus.
★ **Monolithic** — You have one brand which covers everything and commits to a single idea.

This approach allows you to channel your energy and investment but can be more risky. If it goes wrong… then it goes wrong!

How do you evaluate your brand's success? You can review both behaviour and value created for a balanced image of your performance. Value-based success is based on numbers which make it easier to measure. It boils down to your number of customers, frequency of buying, revenue and average spending — simple!

**A behavioural approach is more complex as you measure across five different criteria:**

1. **Awareness** — Are customers aware of your brand? Could they name your company from brand symbols, colour and other visual cues?
2. **Consideration** — When a customer wants your product or services, does your brand come into their mind? For example, most people immediately think of Heinz when they want ketchup.
3. **Preference** — Do customers select you over your customers and why do they prefer your offering?
4. **Satisfaction** — Do you receive many complaints or returns? Your success can be measured by your performance in pleasing customers.
5. **Loyalty** — How many customers make repeat sales and at what level?

Once you begin to assess these points, you are building and measuring your brand equity.

## 1.4  WHY BRAND?

Considered, well-executed branding can improve your organisation's commercial value. If people think highly of your brand, they will be willing to pay a premium for it. If you become a leading brand, you can command a higher price for your product or service and it sets the benchmark for the rest of the market. Branding is a tool used to give yourself a competitive advantage. Therefore, if you want to improve your attractiveness — branding is key! This perceived worth is called "brand equity".

We touched on measuring using a behavioural approach in the last section. Yet, let's delve deeper! You can measure your brand equity via the "Brand Asset Valuator" method by

Young & Rubicam (Y&R). They are an internationally known advertising agency that set out to measure 8,000 local brands and 450 global brands to gain insight into what makes a strong brand. They surveyed nearly 200,000 consumers across the globe using four different measures (Pahud de Mortanges and Van Riel, 2003).

**The four sets of measures (also known as the "Four Pillars of Brand Equity") are:**

- ★ **Knowledge:** this measures the public's understanding of what the brand stands for and what they do.
- ★ **Esteem:** this measures how highly regarded the brand is held by the public. It's closely related to the recognised quality. Is the brand seen as the best in its category?
- ★ **Relevance:** this measures how appropriate the brand is in the current climate and trends.
- ★ **Differentiation:** this measures uniqueness. Highly individual brands are underdogs or are making waves by setting themselves apart from competitors.

When we compare a combination of these measures, we can gain insight into how the audience perceives different brands.

**Knowledge + Esteem = Stature**

The combination of good brand knowledge and esteem can lead to stature. This is your reputation and prestige. Brands that have strong stature are usually ones which have been around for some time. They've made strong brand decisions in the past and have now gained loyalty and clout.

**Relevance + Differentiation = Salience**

The combination of relevance and differentiation will lead to a strong brand. Brand strength is how likely the brand is to succeed in the future. The strongest brands are current and forward-thinking. They are obsessed with their customers and willing to continue innovating to solve customer problems.

Brands that measure highly in both stature and strength are your giants. These are the organisations that everyone knows and (arguably) loves. These include household names such as Apple, Amazon and Google. They are leaders within their markets. An aspirational place to be, indeed!

On the other hand, brands low in stature and strength are usually beginning their lives. They are finding their feet in the market. If your brand is short of strength and stature, it's time to think about your value proposition. You need to communicate key ways you are unique from your competitors to increase differentiation. It's also worth researching current trends and the climate to stay appropriate and boost your relevance.

Now, it may take time to build the "Knowledge" pillar. After all, it requires long-term marketing and advertising strategies to spread awareness of you and your organisation. In the meantime, focus on that value proposition and why you are relevant. Brands that measure high in strength, but low in stature, are growing or niche brands. These include Grammarly and Sweaty Betty.

Brands high in stature, but low in strength are declining within their marketplace. They may be losing out to new, emerging brands and discounters. They have lost their way and become irrelevant to customers leaving them uninspired. This is why it's so important to be progressive and keep your finger on the pulse.

This book will help you build a focused brand, cultivating confidence, so you can resonate with fans. You'll be seen as both relevant and unique. Once your brand identity and strategy are formed, it will be time to implement it! We've also provided guidance on the activation of your brand so you can spread awareness and increase your esteem. Ultimately, if you take care of your brand, your brand will take care of your business and audience.

Many people protest against this sense of mass consumerism which surrounds brands. They cry: "We have become slaves to brands — we must return to a simpler life". We believe this is impossible, brands are here to stay, and they're an essential catalyst for self-expression. Not everyone wants to be a walking billboard for Louis Vuitton or Supreme — and this is good — there's a brand for the minimalists too. Muji is a Japanese brand which translates to "no brand". Brands have power and there is one out there for everyone.

The allure of a brand can be unavoidable. They appeal to our human condition — our need to belong. We all belong, whether it's to a family, religion, or community group. There are even brands for people who feel they don't belong. We use brands to describe our views, personality, aspirations and beliefs.

As Aristotle (supposedly) once said "the soul never thinks without an image". Why do we call it our mind's eye? Because we're visual people. We consume imagery, signs, symbols, and logos. Brands become the object of our consumption, they visualise ideologies and beliefs. Remember, an organisation with no visual language has no identity. In turn, they are boring and instantly forgettable. Can you name a brand with no identity?

When you consider branding, you can minimise risk and increase your security through branding. Consumers and employees commit to brands as they fulfil our essential emotional need to love and belong. Employees who resonate with their brand want to do more and this increases business opportunities. There is a decreased risk for the customer and the business because a brand identity can communicate trust, professionalism, and quality. The union of business, employees, and customers results in growth. Markets love growth prospects.

## *1.5*   BUILDING BRAND CASTLES

Castle. Also known by the name of fortress, keep, or palace. Overall, the structure is there for protection. We see branding providing this same fortification for your own business.

We know first-hand the strength a brand can provide. By building a brand, we were able to go incognito and share our work without the fear of being found out! Buttercrumble acted as a pseudonym. It was our shield and castle. As painfully shy teenagers, we just felt safer developing our creative portfolio like this. We pushed ourselves further. We took risks.

It gave us confidence, and that's important in business. Confidence is a feeling you can adopt for yourself and others. For us, it meant we believed in our ability to achieve success because we'd already accomplished building an identity which we wholeheartedly believed in. In turn, this improved the confidence others had in us. They could be sure about our abilities and qualities because we'd explicitly demonstrated them through Buttercrumble. The brand expressed who we were in an engaging way.

The day you set up a business, you take a risk. You then continue taking risks every day, with every decision. It's exciting, nerve-racking and often eye-opening. Sometimes, it can be overwhelming, but that's OK. If you're thinking about making the "right" move, then good — you care! It is also clear you're pushing boundaries, leaving your comfort zone and making progress.

A lack of confidence is the number one reason why we see business owners holding themselves back. When we have confidence, we are ready for (nearly) anything. We feel like we can move forward and embrace opportunities, rather than run away. If things go wrong, we shrug it off and learn from it. Whereas low confidence means you avoid trying. When a failure occurs, you bury your head in the sand, procrastinate, and prevent yourself from reaching your full potential. You have so much goodness to present to the world, so it's almost criminal to hamper this.

We appreciate it can be hard work carrying all the risk on your shoulders. However, a brand can make decision-making easier. Your brand guidelines act as a compass to help steer the ship. So, shake off the self-doubt, and build your brand! You're ready for it, and we believe in you.

When you create a brand, you can let your business be its amazing self. You take time to appreciate your talents and elevate them. You can even showcase quirks, as this is part of where authenticity derives from. It's what makes you and your offering unique.

## CASE STUDY — FRESHLY MADE

We adopted this same ethos with one of our early identity projects, a local café. The client avoided marketing themselves like the plague. It was a business she'd inherited and was ashamed of its status. She was adamant about describing it as "just a greasy spoon". A greasy spoon is a dingy, cheap restaurant that serves low-quality, high-cholesterol food. This was totally the wrong description, and we had to make our client see sense! Otherwise, it'd be a tragic injustice to our town.

Our shared vision was that it was a community hub for the neighbourhood and a comfortable destination for passing tradespeople. It was in a convenient location, there was complimentary parking, and the space was airy. The café was always spotlessly clean, and the food was fresh. If you wanted a sandwich, they'd make it bespoke for you with a heartfelt touch! You couldn't deny the quality of service, and this needed to be reflected in the identity. We transformed the brand so it was presented as the local, friendly deli as all food is freshly prepared daily for its loyal fans. By reconsidering the strategy, logo design and colour palette, we could make a huge impact with little disruption.

The new identity spurred a total interior renovation and inspired the owner's marketing efforts. Suddenly, she was not promoting a greasy spoon. She was sharing a community destination that she could be proud of. Moreover, the identity makeover proved to her customers that she cared about the business, and was willing to put the effort in. It created a flurry of renewed interest that has further boosted the client's confidence. A huge win!

That said, things can go wrong. If you do make a questionable choice (we've all done it) it's not you with an egg on your face. Suddenly, there's a shield. It's no longer personal — it is about the brand. Any knock-backs just become part of that development and journey. "Character building" if you must. Although, do be careful. You want to protect and nurture your brand, so it's something you're genuinely proud of.

Another word of caution — branding is not a magic wand! Audiences can still have unexpected responses in the face of a carefully cultivated brand image. For example, there have been countless in-person events where we have been asked questions including: "What college are you studying at?" And "Is this your hobby or a full-time job?".

Can you believe this happens in professional sales meetings too? We've received confessions such as "I thought to myself — am I going to work with these young girls? I think I am!" Talk about a backhanded compliment!

We are conscientious of the prejudice minority business owners face and this is why we strive to present ourselves most professionally. Your brand is a great shield, but it can't do everything. Stay resilient and ignore the naysayers.

## ABIGAIL'S REFLECTION

**❝** When I compare our fifteen-year-old selves to ourselves at twenty-five, we would have never pushed ourselves to top brands like Disney. Buttercrumble, as a brand, has allowed us to do this. We ventured down from Leeds to London to deliver a bespoke illustration on a whim after exchanging email conversations with one of Disney's marketing managers. For this story, we'll call her Sarah.

It was a blustery, grey and grim day in the Capital. Great British weather at its best. I remember we had to quickly brush our hair outside, before entering the head office. Yes, Buttercrumble gave us fortification, but we still need to act as polished ambassadors! "Just act confident; like we know what we're doing," I tell Chloe. We enter, following each other through the revolving doors.

We smile at reception, handing a red parcel over to the clerk. "Hello, we're here to drop this parcel off to Sarah within marketing. Please may you pass this on?" Then, the receptionist informed us that they were unable to transfer the post to the rest of the building.

"Yikes!" We thought. We had travelled all this way for nothing.

"Don't worry! I can phone Sarah to come down and collect it personally" the receptionist said, with a phone in hand. "Does Sarah know you? What are your names?"

We respectfully answered and waited. Although Sarah did know us, we weren't sure what she would think regarding our unexpected appearance. Luckily for us, the phone kept on ringing.

"I'm sorry. Sarah must be out for lunch at the moment. I am not supposed to do this, but I can provide you with the address for our post room" the receptionist advised, passing us a map and instructions.

We had to leave the building, walk around the block, locate a garage and enter through a side door. It was dark, concrete and cluttered with warehouse shelving. We wondered if we were even in the right place! Luckily, we found a hatch at the end of the room. We peered through to discover Disney's postman with bags of packages and letters.

He looked surprised. Perhaps he didn't receive many visitors? Nonetheless, we quickly passed him our red parcel, thanked him and made a quick getaway. Mission accomplished.

Admittedly, we're still developing our relationships with our contacts at Disney, but this helped us make an impact. You will get yourself out there more when you are proud of your brand. We're always planning our next publicity stunt. After all, it's for the good of the business!

. . . . . . . . . . . . . . . . . .

BUTTERCRUMBLE.

~~~~~~~~~~~~~~~~~~~~~~~~~~~~~~~~~~~~~~~~~~~~~~~~~~~~~~

<     *Left, top logo: our identity pre-2015. It's bubbly and fun which reflects the designs we love to create. A heart motif, "Butter" and "Crumble" are stacked, but this caused confusion when people wrote our business name. "Buttercrumble" is one word, a portmanteau.*

*Left, bottom logo: our latest logo. It shows "Buttercrumble" written in rounded lettering, punctuated by a heart motif. It's simple, yet friendly! The heart also acts as confident brand mark. It's an evolution based on our previous design.*

# Chapter 2

# STRATEGIC BRAND ANALYSIS

*Use your peripheral vision*

---

## *2.1* COMPETITOR ANALYSIS

When you run a business, it becomes an obsession. You can obsess about your competitors, your workflow and your bottom line. This focus will help you survive. Yet, obsessing about your customers can take you even further.

When you watch Olympians race the 100m sprint, where are they looking? They're certainly not staring at each other. They stay in their lane and keep their eyes on the prize — the finishing line. If they glance to the left or right, it will only slow them down. It's one reason why racing horses wear blinkers. Keep your attention dedicated to what's ahead of you.

Instead, sprinters can use their peripheral vision. They can remain focused whilst assessing "Do I have company?" Or "Is there a gap?" They are then able to decide how to run the rest of their race (all in a matter of seconds).

Fortunately, as a business owner or brand manager, you have more time. You can analyse your competitors to help you assess the overall field, yet it's the customers you should be paying attention to. If you can consistently listen to them and solve their problems, then they will take care of your business. If customers are always at the heart, they will select you again and again. Suddenly, you're not so worried about what your rivals are doing! You have your loyal clan and you're able to rely on one another.

We like to "be more Olympian", but we're no strangers to competition research. We've been at the receiving end of awkward questioning. Yes, another agency asked for our yearly turnover target at a networking event. We were astonished — firstly it's uncustomary in Britain to discuss financials — did they think we were going to divulge our details to strangers? The sharing of commercially sensitive information with competitors is risky business. It can reduce the incentive to compete, to the detriment of customers in the long run.

At the discovery stage of a project, we will usually ask businesses about their aspirations. We'll question them about brands they admire and ones they dislike. However, we are sometimes met with contempt. They are worried about copying others and that they will be another clone company.

However, your brand's position can not be decided in isolation! You need to consider its role within the context of other competitor brands. If you create a "brandscape", you can discover your route to market. You'll find your space within the field. For those concerned about being influenced, it's good to remember that originality is not the generation of "something" out of "nothing". We use inputs from this amazing world around us. By twisting conventions, we create something extraordinary from the ordinary. Use history as a lesson to learn what works and what doesn't. There's so much to be understood from research.

Most people establish a business based on their own experience and knowledge. It's just like the age-old saying "Write what you know". When you're basing your business on an existing skill, you have already accomplished a large chunk of research. You may even already be an expert — fantastic! Use this to your advantage.

Moreover, our studies placed us in a great position when understanding our competitors. We were always looking at other illustrators and designers, they informed our work, and we had to demonstrate our research skills.

Keep a sketchbook, notebook, or log and look at the world around you. Which businesses do you like or dislike? Why? What do they do well? What could they do better? There are no right or wrong answers, but by putting in the groundwork, you can create a unique formula for your business.

## ABIGAIL'S REFLECTION

**❝** Most people set up businesses within the industries they have experience. So, your competitor analysis has already begun. When starting Buttercrumble, I was no expert, but I did have a couple of years behind me from working in a digital marketing agency. I am always so grateful for the time I spent here, and to the team for taking a chance on me. By working on real briefs, I learnt at a faster pace than I did at university. I also discovered how agencies operate. This was the start of Buttercrumble's competitor analysis. I learnt the tone of client communication, how to multi-task on a range of projects and how to present oneself. If you find yourself in this situation, keep notes and learn from each day. You'll find golden nuggets of information which you'd struggle to read in a business book.

· · · · · · · · · · · · · · · · · ·

## CHLOE'S REFLECTION

**❝** From 2014 to 2016 I put the academic research skills I'd learnt to good use… by promoting our competition! Oh no! But, in all seriousness, I had little to no business intentions, I just loved graphic design. I joined the illustration website Illustration Friday (now Illustration Age) as a writer. My role was voluntary and each month, I would find an illustrator to interview, request their participation, and write up their responses. I asked the questions. I sought the answers. Now I can look back and see what a crucial exercise this was. It is notoriously difficult to find success as an illustrator and I found that what you needed was a strong personal brand and commercial mindset.

During this time, I also started working at a public relations agency which gave me a deeper insight into the creative world and business. I think industry experience is crucial in providing a practical understanding. By working within another agency I could see how the structure and hierarchy of teams worked, the process of welcoming new clients, and account management. My colleagues were constantly on the phones, catching up with executives and decision-makers, and ensuring everything was running smoothly. I admired this attention to detail and customer service — this personal approach is something we've adapted within our own business. Another aspect which inspired us was the agency's specialism, they focused on what they knew, loved, and did best. By curating a specific client base, they not only make their clients feel special, but they could demonstrate their expertise and passion for a certain industry. Again, what can you learn from your past experiences and employers? If they're in a similar field to where you're heading, they can be a helpful point of guidance.

In 2016, we completed our enterprise scholarship and degree in graphic and communication design, and I knew it was time to shake off the blogging and focus on putting my design skills to good use. I had dedicated hours to research and my mind was fit to burst. I continued to work with the PR agency, before working in-house for a crafting company. By 2017, I knew I had the expertise and training to go forth and build a business we could be proud of.

. . . . . . . . . . . . . . . . . . .

## 2.2   CUSTOMER ANALYSIS

You can't understand someone until you've walked a mile in their shoes. Countless professionals and experts stress the importance of customer profiling. How can you expect to sell to someone if you don't understand their needs? We think this is a skill that takes time, after all, it takes time to walk that mile.

The formation of Buttercrumble was so organic that we never really profiled our customers in the early days. We created our first business plan, in 2015, which contained the generic profile of a small business owner. This was a good start as our plan showed empathy. The result — it helped to secure our scholarship — an important business milestone for us.

Although it's not always essential to partake in lengthy profiling exercises, you should always keep your customer in mind. Ongoing customer analysis enabled us to spot a clear pattern emerging in our customer base. Our playful blend of illustration and graphic design, like no other, attracted family end-consumers.

To test this theory, we attended Bubble London. At the time, Bubble London was the leading premium kidswear and lifestyle brands trade show. The show has now recently been relaunched as part of Pure London. We spent the two days completing brand activations such as illustrating portraits of visitors and delivering a design seminar. What an opportunity and experience. It was great to share the value of visuals with an audience of children's brand owners, and we received fantastic feedback. Although we didn't generate direct business on the day, we cultivated a vital network of the businesses we love.

It makes sense to repeat success so, as a result of Bubble London, we began to plan our trip to Playtime Paris. Picaflor's Playtime Paris is another premium trade show, dedicated to children and maternity. In January 2019, we attended the global show which saw an incredible 7235 visitors over the three days. A striking 56.7% of those were international according to Playtime's show report (February 2019) and this clarified our target audience even more! From the event, we could recognise the global opportunities for our audience and we generated new business from the show.

Playtime Paris also enabled us to scale up our live illustration service — quite literally! We created a giant group portrait of the event's attendees. The mural was inspired by Playtime Paris' theme of "family" and encouraged participation. We were able to encourage visitors to engage with the arts and boost positivity. Illustration has the power to boost wellbeing and spark the imagination and we wanted to allow visitors and exhibitors to experience this to nurture the show's positive vibes. It was an accessible and engaging activity so we could engage as many people as possible.

We continue to develop, evaluate, and refine our customer profile. We pivot our brand to meet our customer's pain points and ensure we are providing the remedies they need. This is all whilst staying authentic and true to Buttercrumble's values and vision. We are strong believers in evolution over revolution. If you want to grow a brand customers know and trust, they must get to know you and build familiarity. By swapping and changing too regularly, you may confuse customers. It is possible to change for the better whilst maintaining trust with those who know your brand.

Whether we're working with our own brand or our client's brands, we write a customer persona/profile. You will want to include all the nitty-gritty information and don't be afraid to visualise this. A persona is our go-to foundation when thinking about customers so what does this entail?

Try to focus on envisioning one person in your mind. There is no reason why you can't create more than one persona but let's keep it simple — one at a time. Start with a general overview, what's their name, where do they live, and what's their demographic? (We tend to refer to NRS social grades as they're widely used and give an instant impression of occupation and class). Determine their gender and age. Can you describe their career and how this fits within their lifestyle? What do their day-to-day activities look like? Delve a little deeper into their personality and values as these emotional qualities heavily influence our buying habits. If you think your persona is too generic or you're struggling to describe these emotional attributes, you could list their favourite magazines, brands, and celebrities. This information will also offer a clue to where you might find your customer, don't forget to mention the online world as well as the physical world. Finally, and perhaps most importantly, discuss the customer's pain points and consider how you would remedy these.

Once you've analysed your customer, it's time to dive into the meat and potatoes, you can create a satisfying and robust marketing strategy. You may be familiar with the popular "Concept of the Marketing Mix" by Neil H. Borden (1964). The professor of marketing defined ingredients to evaluate how to promote a brand's offering, these have since been refined to the "4 Ps of Marketing", and are:

★ **Product:** A product can also cover intangible services — it does not need to be a physical good. The important thing is that it fulfils the needs or desires of consumers. It may seem simplistic but it's crucial you clearly define your offering before you can market it.

★ **Price:** To define your price, you need to calculate your supply, demand, marketing plan and your desired profit margins. Furthermore, you need to price and position yourself strategically against other brands.

★ **Promotion:** How does your consumer learn about your product? Promotion can include advertising, public relations, social media marketing, search engine optimisation and email marketing to name a few.

★ **Place:** Where can customers reach your product? Where do your customers shop? You need to select the places your customers visit to convert sales. These can be physical brick-and-mortar places or within the digital realms.

This concept can be a great tool when trying to market to your target audience. Look at each P and explore how it relates to your customer. Start with your product (or service) and question what it is your customer actually wants or needs. What are their pain points and how does your product or service remedy them?

With price in mind, what is the perceived value of your product or service and can you use this to differentiate from your competitors? If your marketplace is saturated, you may use price to position yourself at the extremes of the market. You could be super-competitive, competitively or as a luxury innovator.

Promotion explores how your customers interact with your brand. You need to ask yourself (or your customers) their preferred channel of communication. Social media may be the perfect platform to promote your products… or do your customers rely on the recommendations of their friends and relatives? Some people look to magazines whilst radio marketing may be a personal touch-point for local customers.

Finally, where can customers find your product? Do you sell to businesses, or direct to consumers? This may affect where you place your product. For example, trade shows are great to sell to retail buyers or within specialist industries. Alternatively, you may choose to select boutiques at a higher price point.

There is no exact science to combining these ingredients but they should serve as a guide. Manage your judgement and experience to create the best mix for your customers and don't be afraid to evaluate, adapt and develop your offerings.

Have fun when analysing and creating your audience base — but don't get caught up in a fairytale of someone who doesn't exist — try and avoid assumptions. Stereotypes can hold some truth but you don't want to create a clichéd view of your customers. This could prevent you from creating real connections or even acknowledging a more suitable market segment.

## BE CURIOUS

Whilst consulting a luxury accessories brand, we realised the whole team made an assumption. We assumed an older demographic (females in their fifties) is more likely to buy from luxury brands. Our initial reaction didn't account for the lifestyle of the audience.

It makes more sense to look at the income bracket of customers when exploring the best target audience for luxury goods; age is not a guaranteed indicator of income. For example, today there's a rising middle class among different generations including those in their thirties; they're the modern Yuppie! Professor of Public Policy, Short (1989) refers to the "mythological" Yuppie, a stereotype of the 1980s boom, they were the young-professional and city-slicker. It should be noted that this was a myth as many countries faced an economic slump. Fast-forward to today, we can see new yuppies as a real audience, proving stereotypes are problematic. Our world cities are securing their positions as powerhouses and homes to affluent young professionals — traditional demographics are changing.

On reflection, if you take lifestyle into account, it all makes perfect sense. Many people in their fifties are absorbing the cost of raising and educating their children, they may still be paying their mortgage or other financial contracts. You need to consider their employment status and household size before making snap judgements. They are more likely to have disposable income as they enter their late fifties and beyond.

We decided to focus on ladies in their late fifties in addition to a younger audience. We created a segment of young professionals in their thirties with no children and a passion for travel to convert more sales.

**So, how do you avoid making assumptions when completing your customer profile?**

★ **Combine research sources:** Don't get hooked on one exciting piece of data. Be critical of the evidence and dig deeper to identify any blind spots.

★ **Avoid stereotypes:** I cannot stress the importance of questions. Don't just take information for granted, acknowledge the assumption, then see if it's right. Ask other people their opinion and back up your thoughts with data.

★ **Understand lifestyle:** Go deeper than age, sex, and profession. You need to develop a deeper understanding of how your customer lives their day-to-day life. Consider their online landscape, which magazines they read, and which programmes they watch.

Never underestimate the power of thoughtful customer analysis. It takes time to do the research, and it takes time to trial your ideas, but it's a long-term investment. Customers are valuable marketing tools, there is no better marketing than a positive word-of-mouth recommendation.

A focused analysis will increase your efficiency and maximise results. However, we do have a cautionary tale for those who are too restricted in their audience choices! We love a strong fable and the story of the egg maid is no exception… The egg maid would carry the daily production of eggs to market in a single basket, preoccupied with daydreams about how she'd spend her earnings, she clumsily dropped the basket. Unfortunately, all the eggs broke and she was left with nothing! Oh, if she had split the production between two baskets, half of her dreams may have come true. It's a classic case of "don't put all your eggs in one basket".

This was especially true for us during the COVID-19 pandemic. At Buttercrumble, we focus on the cultural sector and retailers. This was a problem once lock-down and social distancing commenced. All galleries, museums and shops were shut. To offer solutions,

# CUSTOMER PROFILE

*Activity*

—

**Name:**
..................................................

Illustrate or attach a photograph of your customer

**Age:**
..................................................

**Gender:**
..................................................

**Career:**
..................................................

**Personality:**
..................................................

..................................................

**Values:**
..................................................

..................................................

**Lifestyle:**
..................................................

**Favourite publications, brands and celebrities:**
..................................................

..................................................

**Social media usage:**
..................................................

..................................................

**Pain points:**
..................................................

..................................................

we supported these organisations with digital outreach. This helped them to connect with their audience in engaging ways using technology. Yet our clients were rightfully concerned about the impact of investing in anything new at such a precarious time. People don't spend in times of uncertainty. Projects slowed down or were placed on hiatus. This could have been disastrous for our business if we hadn't had a backup plan!

Fortunately, we have always stayed true to our "young-at-heart" vibes. This means we're able to appeal to a wider market. We appeal to those organisations who want to target families. This included children's brands. During the pandemic, we were able to secure three sizable contracts for this segment which was a relief and joy! We were still able to collaborate on projects we loved because our brand meant we were still attracting like-minded companies.

It is still essential to have focus so your messaging is clear and captivating. Nonetheless, there are times when you need to use your creativity to think outside of the box. During economic recessions, you have to be able to innovate and adapt. Be open to the possibilities. If a particular audience is struggling — support them! Once they are back on their feet, they'll remember the help you provided. If they are not spending, you can look further afield to find other ways to sell.

## 2.3   YOUR BRAND ANALYSIS

To guarantee lasting success, one must analyse and evaluate their brand. Even if your brand is relatively new, you can examine results as you progress. This will help you to craft an authentic and effective brand identity and strategy.

Start by separating your brand image, strategy and identity:

★ **Brand image:** the audience's general perception and impression of the organisation.
★ **Brand strategy:** the core values, advantages, personality and mission that the organisation sets.

★ **Brand identity:** the visual language of your brand. Such as logo design, typography and colour palette.

You may have a desired brand image in mind but it's a matter of external opinion. You can only hope to influence perceptions through a thoughtfully crafted brand identity and strategy. To be successful, you must consider how you'd like your audience to feel by determining their values. You can use this to steer your identity and strategy decisions.

Brand strategy can be led by external or internal forces. External forces include the brand, customers, and finance. The most important things to externally-focused organisations are building a culture and idea in the minds of customers, understanding these customers and their needs, and growing shares within the business.

Internally-focused brands are concerned with their purpose, products and employees. For example, they might be driven to "do good" for the planet, push product and technology development, or maximise their employee experience.

Your external and internal lens can be a good starting point when defining your brand strategy. You can build upon these foundations to develop an authentic and meaningful personality.

You can also commence your brand strategy by reflecting on history, culture, and traditions. Past case studies can grant fruitful insights into best-practice. Why learn from your own mistakes when you can learn from others?

For example, the Quaker business culture holds a certain fascination with us. It's said the faith was born in England during the 17th Century (when many Quakers were persecuted for their beliefs) they formed a close-knit community for protection and trust. Quakers were supported by their communities and this empowered them to find new ways of doing business. They brought new standards of honesty, truth and integrity to business practices. This escalated their success as people knew they could trust Quakers with their hard-earned cash. The whole community worked together to maintain high levels of trust, transparency, and financial security. Furthermore, they cared for equality and ensured business relationships were fair.

Buttercrumble resonates with this wholesome approach to business and appreciates the power of community. Like many Quaker businesses, Buttercrumble is a family affair, and this support network has been crucial to our success. Our business is closely invested in our personal beliefs and attitudes. We have a genuine interest in our industry based on our own experiences which, in some ways, makes branding easier. We can talk as "Buttercrumble" with ease because we are the brand. It's ingrained in our being and the business felt inevitable. After all, before we had the intelligence and self-awareness to question our identities, we had already inherited one.

This culture's long-lasting success is clear as many Quaker-founded companies still exist today including: Clarks Shoes, Lloyds, Barclays, Cadburys, Frys, Western Union and Rowntrees.

Once you've conducted your research, you must continue to review your brand to stay relevant and successful. Here are some questions to consider when analysing your brand:

What are the values of your audience and how do these compare to your own? As a business leader, you need to feel motivated by your brand (and so does your team). Find where your values and your audience's values overlap. This shared interest is how you can connect on an emotional level with your customers.

Do you know what your audience thinks of you? Ask them! But, be a critical thinker. You must remain balanced when listening to the opinions of others. Be someone who is reflective and can evaluate the reasoning behind a statement or decision. You suspect everything and this becomes a cause for change.

It's easier than ever to reach your audience. If you're unable to sit down and chat with your customers over a coffee (some brands still do this) then consider setting up a small virtual focus group. Moreover, this is a great way to build rapport with your most loyal and valued supporters.

When building Buttercrumble, many well-meaning people offered their own opinion. Along the way, we've received the best, timeless advice and a few curveballs too. However, some advice can be disruptive and non-applicable. If you feel the advice is bestowed with bad timing, in the wrong context, or with misunderstanding — refer back to your values.

You'll learn when to take action and when to take advice with a pinch of salt. The same can be said with the guidance we are offering. Although we are brand guardians, this is no gospel truth! It's our experience of developing a home-grown brand.

Are you following a clear vision? Don't be embarrassed to want something. If we break free from the fear of criticism and failure regarding our vision, we can focus on striving toward our wildest dreams. The fearless are wild and those who dare, win. When we use our imagination, the possibilities are endless.

With a clear vision, your brand will blossom. The process should feel organic and natural, after all, you simply cannot demand a flower to bloom overnight! Instead, you can command love and focus.

Our vision has driven us since being college students living at home with our parents. Watching Buttercrumble flower over time has been an absolute joy; it's grown with us and therefore feels genuine. A vision has strengthened our character and resilience — personally and in business — Buttercrumble is one tough cookie! When building your brand, we hope you can feel this same instinct to nurture your vision.

What are your strengths, weaknesses, opportunities and threats? Use the dependable SWOT framework to help identify the strategic position of your organisation within the business landscape. By listing strengths, weaknesses, opportunities and threats, you can find a direction to move forward in. It will help you build upon what you do well, minimise risks and tackle any challenges. It's a tried-and-tested way of optimising success. This activity is a no-brainer for any business.

Once you've conducted your research, you have a strong foundation of knowledge which can help inform your future branding decisions. Any confusion can be clarified and you can feel confident in the solutions you're offering as a business.

Think "Olympian" when you're conducting analysis. It's essential to stay curious, but don't let others distract you. Use your peripheral vision and do not take your eyes off that finish line! Go for gold! We believe in you!

< *Locals frequently ask about the branding we created for The Little Bookshop. The Leeds-based store has flourished since 2017, and we couldn't be more thrilled for the team.*

*We had a lovely time creating an illustrative identity. The application was across many touchpoints; this helped it come to life.*

# Chapter 3

# THE BRAND'S CORE

*Make it powerful.*

———————

Insipid, passive brands leave themselves open to attacks. A genuine personality can offer your brand protection from copy-cats as it cannot be easily replicated. Imitators may steal your product attributes but they can't steal what's intangible. Personality is at the core of your brand and it needs to be strong enough to support the superficial elements of your organisation.

In life and business, one can't just chop and change their personality. By the age of thirty, character is usually set in concrete. Just think about a time you tried to reinvent yourself… It seems like a great idea at first, but you usually find yourself slipping into old habits. Your brand's personality is your organisation's biggest commitment.

Authenticity has reliable sticking powers and, in business, you have to stay true to yourself.

Consider enhancing your brand's personality to help you develop a powerful identity.

❝ There was a time when I would cringe whenever anyone asked what our business was called. "Buttercrumble", I'd say meekly. This always (and still now) lead to eyebrow-raising responses. "Oo, it sounds delicious" or "It reminds me of biscuits and all things sweet". All brilliantly positive comments! I'd rather evoke a reaction than blend into the background. Now, I embrace it as a strong and memorable brand asset. The moral is, doing be afraid to be left-field or think outside of the box. Often, we're too embarrassed to push boundaries because we may look silly. "What if people talk?" We say let 'em! It's free advertising.

· · · · · · · · · · · · · · · · · ·

Your brand's core should be formed of distinctive values. These can be punchy statements which inform your guiding principles (more on these later!). Your values translate as a compass for your business decisions. They will help you to foster the right culture and build a team of amazing, like-minded individuals.

Core values are intrinsic and come from within. You cannot force others to share your values — people simply do or don't — you need to find your tribe. Then, you must retain this talent by staying true to your core values. Values must be extracted (and not feigned) due to their innate quality. You already know your values! You just need to put them on paper… Easy, right? Nu-uh.

It can be tricky to articulate something inborn and intangible. When you live and breathe the brand, so much of what you do is a journey of discovery. You create, experiment and test ideas to find a sense of harmony.

Make the first step by placing a piece of blank paper in front of you and — without over-thinking — write down your values. Then, write down the problem your business is solving, and what success ultimately looks like.

Most importantly, ask yourself why? Why (as a brand) do you do what you do? Customers are attracted to a brand's authentic passion for their product or service — they want to understand your values. Another way to consider this question is by asking yourself "What would my business never do?"

When we think about success, we think of community. We wanted to share our love of creativity with other design enthusiasts around the world and feel connected. A brand enabled us to do this because it provided a meaningful platform for us to share this passion (without being too "me, me, me"). We understand that it's frustrating for others when they have an idea they want to share, but don't know how. Yet, we can help. We believe that if creation is possible, then nothing is impossible. When we make things for others, we want them to feel understood. It's about expressing their vision, and the community is formed around this.

Other examples of brand values could include "we value honesty", "we prioritise families" or "we respect our teammates".

A brand helps you to visualise success, and what it may mean to you (and or your business). Sometimes, it can feel overwhelming to take a blank page and express what success means, as it means so many different things at different stages of our lives. Priorities can change, and that's OK. Still, considering a mission and vision can make things feel more achievable. It provides structure.

The mission is what you do each day to reach your vision — the big success. Please note, you'll find it's not just about the destination, it's about the journey. It may be a cheesy statement, but it's true.

Once you've filled your paper with ramblings, pin them on your fridge, and mull them over. These will form your core values. After a week, you can finesse no more than five brand values which you can commit to. Any more than this is unrealistic as you (and your team) will struggle to recall them. Plus, too much time is spent drafting values and mission statements. Their purpose is not to exist on paper, but to exist through your brand actions which lead to success.

As mentioned, core values come from within, they must be true to your brand's character. If you look at these values and don't see them projected on your social media, in your stores, or through your people… you need to rethink! Use your true values to deliver meaningful results to your customers and clients, teammates, and suppliers. Attract like-minded wonders and start to build your brand's community.

Ultimately, you must create a distinctive personality and identity for your brand. It is more effective at communicating your product's benefits than directly stating such benefits exist since it enhances likeability and authenticity.

## *3.1* MISSION

**Know your mission and make it powerful.**

We decided to stay true to ourselves when cultivating Buttercrumble's core and, this means, we have to challenge the perceptions of a design "agency". We found this to be somewhat of a dirty word to our smaller clients, although it really shouldn't be. Nonetheless, we're all about our people and it didn't feel fitting for Buttercrumble. We are more than those negative perceptions, we are an empowering ethos. We offer a new approach to design through our positivity, co-design, and personal touches. There's a creative revolution in our midst, and we want to ride that wave, casting our fairy dust through playful branding. Essentially, Buttercrumble's mission is to set businesses' stages for magic through the power of design.

To create a mission is to define your story within one succinct statement. Your brand's mission is a vital ingredient for creating a coherent brand. This mission will give you a deeper understanding of your brand, which in turn, will cultivate your audience's loyalty and trust. We present to you the essential questions in your mission formula. Answer these and see your brand take shape...

What's Your Purpose: A purpose is the reason for which something is done or created or for which something exists. What was your objective in setting up your business? For example, The Coca-Cola Company was founded to "Refresh the world. Make a difference" (2020). Punchy!

### How Do You Achieve Your Purpose?

Time to get practical. The Coca-Cola Company refreshes the world by providing beverages to consumers globally and they do this using sustainable practices which make a difference in people's lives, communities and our planet. Are you serving your local community with professional cleaning services? Or selling unique wares from independent artists and makers? Perhaps you are the proud owner of a holistic care home.

### Who For?

Think about your customer, your team, and yourself. Who does the business benefit?

### Why You?

This is the secret ingredient, it can be your unique selling point, why should you be the one to carry out this mission? It's a competitive market out there, so you need to explain what sets you apart and makes you the perfect choice for your dream customers.

When we think about Buttercrumble and our mission, we know, we are here to empower young-at-heart businesses to express themselves. We create campaigns and identities that make us smile, our clients smile, and in turn, make their customers smile too. Unlike other agencies, we offer a dedicated expert to optimise the experience, evergreen support and a holistic approach to visual story-telling.

Use your answers to craft a mission statement and don't forget to display it in your workspace. It will become a constant reminder of why you are doing this — especially when times get tough. It will not only benefit you, but your team too (if you have one). You and your team can measure your actions against the organisation's brand mission and be committed to making things happen. This is due to the additional direction provided. If your brand has no direction, you and the team may feel misguided and confused about what is to be prioritised. Develop your mission and feel the surge of motivation!

We believe the mission and vision are more natural when the business is founded from a genuine passion for the service or product offering. For example, a mother who discovers a novel way to make meals fun (and thus launches a lunch-bag brand) knows her mission is to maximise quality time for families everywhere. Her vision is that no child will live in hunger or fear of food.

However, an entrepreneur who buys a franchise — because they see a gap in their town for a new takeaway restaurant — may not have the same personal drive as the mother. Now, we might be wrong but we suspect they'll need to think more carefully about the brand's purpose and "big why" to articulate an authentic mission and vision statement. That is if it isn't already outlined in their franchisee guidebook… It hardly feels inspiring.

This said a more pragmatic approach can be beneficial. Investor-entrepreneurs are less likely to be blind in love and can view things more objectively. Some business owners are so passionate about their offering that they can bulldoze over their customers' needs because they assume they know best.

A clear business mission and vision can not only help to connect your brand with customers but with your employees too. When your team understands the brand's purpose and it's synergised with their own identity, they feel motivated because they value the brand's impact. You can enhance this by creating opportunities to enhance your employees' potential. The team can see how the brand's mission and vision will help them to become a better person, expand their learning, and in turn, receive a promotion.

When asking what success looks like to different brand owners we often hear responses such as "to be doing something meaningful" or "have a business which enables my lifestyle". When you think about it, these should be the standards we expect. They will not give you and your team the long-lasting motivation to drive your brand to success. Your mission and vision should be specific and distil the real reason why your brand exists. Only then, will you have a clear direction for your brand.

## 3.2  VISION

As an entrepreneur, colleagues and customers must understand your vision. We understand that a business' vision is created by you, its founder, and once your business grows it should be shared by your team. To inspire everyone, your vision must be more aspirational and rousing than your mission statement. Don't forget to dream big, communicate in the present tense, and keep your words short and sweet.

Aspiration is key. Do you want global offices? Do you want to end world hunger? Do you want to appear on the fashion runways of New York, Paris, Milan and London? If you want to grow a big brand, you need to stop thinking small, think big!

A clear vision will keep your organisation on track. If you feel yourself getting lost, go back to visioning and remind yourself why you're building a brand. Understanding your 'why?' is the key to unlocking your business potential. Your vision must communicate your ultimate reason for being and how the business will look in the future.

This can be summarised in a succinct paragraph by answering two questions:

**How Will You Change The World?**

If your answer doesn't scare you or make you laugh, it's not big enough. TOMS, an ethical shoe company, has a powerful, global vision. They believe everyone has the right to live free of violence and everyone should have the means to realise their full potential, free from stress. Everyone should have equal access to education, a decent income, and good healthcare (2020).

**How Do You Communicate Your Reason for Being?**

TOMS communicates a clear commitment to its vision through donations. For every $3 TOMS makes, they donate $1. They dedicate at least one-third of their net annual profits to their giving fund, which means they can distribute shoes and grants. If you're passionate about sustainability you could pledge to plant trees. Or, maybe you care about equal opportunities and have introduced a pioneering training scheme. You could be a guardian of your local economy by championing your suppliers.

To be successful, you must consider every person involved in your business, not just customers. Show your employees you care about them by involving them in your vision creation and ask them to think about how they will help make the world a better place. There is no use in dreaming up a vision if your team is ignorant, you can work together to achieve your business goals.

A business without focus and soul is a business struggling to inspire its customers. What's driving your company forward? Nurture your vision every, single, day. Then translate this vision from your mind into a reality.

As a business, it's easy to become preoccupied with unexpected changes and opportunities, your time and energy are spent on immediate challenges. As a result, you constantly feel like you're playing catch-up and you become stuck in a vicious cycle.

To have a vision is to be proactive. You can take charge of your organisation's future by anticipating and preparing for changes! Behavioural scientists, Ratiba Bouhali et al. (2015), have identified compelling reasoning for a strategic visionary approach; it provides a stronger awareness of the organisation's weaknesses and needs, helps to define your mission and objectives, provides a greater sense of direction to your team and creates accountability.

We also believe it prevents procrastination and builds momentum. This saved time and energy will create space for other creative pursuits and fruitful business activities.

If you can focus on your vision, values, and mission — rather than corporate fluctuations — you can maintain order. Avoid stressful chaos by staying aligned with your vision and journey towards your dream future.

## 3.3  GUIDING PRINCIPLES

A principle is defined in the dictionary as a "fundamental truth or proposition that serves as the foundation for a system of belief or behaviour or a chain of reasoning" (Lexico Powered by Oxford, 2019). Principles can be seen as laws which help guide an organisation through day-to-day operations.

Sometimes it's fun to break the rules, but your guiding principles should be seen as essential peace-keepers within your organisation. When we abide by these rules, your team and customers will feel a part of a trustworthy, stable environment. They will be comfortable (and even proud) to associate themselves with the organisation.

By having a set of guiding principles, you will retain integrity. Integrity is important within business as it dictates honesty and self-respect. You are not going to delude anyone when you stand by your morals.

Three moral philosophies to review are people, values and rules. When you feel psychologically safe, you can make good decisions based on these. 'People' means you are behaving as a good person would do. You are doing the right thing, first and foremost. It's absolutely clear you care about others! 'Values' contemplates complex decisions using moral values such as courage and justness. 'Rules' are in place to keep yourself and others safe and well (Steare, 2020). Consideration of people, values and rules are the steps you need to take to build an ethically sound organisation. By considering these three moral philosophies, you can craft meaningful guiding principles for your brand. Consumers then know how much your brand genuinely cares.

Examples of your principles could be:

"I will treat my customers as I want to be treated".

"The buck stops here with us".

"Our products use only sustainable materials".

You don't need to have hundreds of principles — it is far better to commit fully to just a couple. These guiding principles will help keep you on track to building a brand with fans. After all, It encourages respect and helps you find a like-minded audience. It will also help you develop organisational values as we move on to developing your brand's unique value proposition.

Your guiding principles, dependent on your organisation, often link to the leader's moral compass. They can be founded over time through experience and we've found this intimate reflection helps to build guiding principles you can truly believe in.

We discovered the importance of "trusting your instincts". Your intuition is a web of feelings hard-wired in your brain, based on your past experiences. Your subconscious directs decision-making and there are a lot of decisions to make in business. At Buttercrumble, we believe partnerships must feel good. Not only must our designs make our clients smile, and their customers smile, they need to make us smile too!

## CHLOE'S REFLECTION

66 Don't be afraid to trust your instincts, they are like your guardian angel, directing you on the right path.

Around 2012, we applied to our chosen university courses, before a little diversion. Abigail applied for architecture due to her love of form, place-making and design. Whilst I applied for fine art and painting courses with a passion to pursue a creative career. But, after months of travelling the country, application submissions, and interviews, we had a change of heart…

The architecture course was too lengthy and structured for Abigail. Fine art was too ambiguous for a practical person like me.

What's more, many of the universities preferred applicants who had attended their foundation courses, as it demonstrated a commitment to the arts. Well, we committed to the arts the first time we put pen to paper! Because of this, we didn't see the extra expense as feasible for our family. Our parents were already sending two of their daughters to expensive universities and we knew we needed to work hard to fund our studies.

Our enjoyment of graphic design at college was growing and we were receiving an increasing number of commissions for our illustrative work. "Let's apply to a graphic design course", we thought. Hence, we both applied to the University of Leeds through UCAS Extra with success. Hindsight is a wonderful thing, if we hadn't enrolled at Leeds, we may not have launched Buttercrumble. The support we received during university was vital to the success of our business.

. . . . . . . . . . . . . . . . . .

Moreover, the community is at the heart of all we do. We genuinely care about nurturing the people in our world as they have helped to elevate us. We show our audience we care by campaigning and advocating for causes close to our hearts. This passion has opened the door to so many exciting opportunities including a visit to the House of Lords.

We couldn't believe our luck when we received the invitation from the British Library who asked us to attend as representatives for small businesses. We were nominated as a nationwide case-study thanks to our connections with Leeds Central Library's Business and IP Centre, and to our disbelief, we were selected. At first, we thought we would be attending alongside a whole host of fantastic enterprises from across the UK but that wasn't to be the case, we were one of a select few.

This was all rather surprising as we even struggled to find the correct entrance to the event (security was rather high) and London always feels somewhat exclusive. The simplest of trips could turn into an adventure for us!

Nonetheless, we wanted to make the most of the rare opportunity to hobnob with key decision-makers and business owners! We stood by the Thames (with a view of the London Eye and Big Ben) as we snacked on our posh granola and wore our Sunday best. Our eyes were open. We really could represent our fellow small businesses and bring awareness to matters we cared about.

The right guiding principles will inspire you and keep you grounded. Look for the experiences which spark your fire.

# Chapter 4

# YOUR UNIQUE VALUE PROPOSITION

*Give the people what they want.*

———————————

In workshops, we often use the analogy of the chocolate truffle and Maltesers (after all, we love sweet things). Both are small, round, brown and delicious. However, each sends out a different message. Maltesers are family-friendly, accessible and of great value. They are regular, so there are no strange surprises. It's a dependable bag of chocolates! On the other hand, chocolate truffles are premium and luxurious. Each is slightly different in shape due to its artisan nature. They are pure indulgence. Of course, there is a place in the world for both of these. Yet, each sets different expectations. In the business landscape, there will be others providing the same basic product or service as you, but how can you differentiate yourself? By finding your unique value proposition.

❝ In one workshop, I questioned participants: "Are you on Team Truffle or Team Malteser?"

One lady said she wanted to be both — great value and premium. However, this can cause a contradiction and can confuse your audience. It's best to develop a consistent tone and messaging for maximum impact, even if you'll displease some groups. If you decide to be on both teams, use harmonious values together for the best effect. For example, both Maltesers and chocolate truffles offer enjoyment and a moment of gratification. Which team do you fancy?

Some organisations can achieve maximum attraction across a range of audiences. However, the cost of this may be boredom. If you were ice cream, you'd probably be vanilla. It's not exactly a unique value proposition. You may have mass appeal, but where are your raving fans?

· · · · · · · · · · · · · · · · · ·

Airbnb, although a strong brand, has suffered from the saturation of trends. Originally, the company proposed to disturb the hotel industry by allowing travellers to stay in the real homes of real people, in real neighbourhoods (Heathcote, 2020). Airbnb's unique value proposition was authenticity. They wanted to offer genuine experiences to backpackers and globetrotters (not tourists).

Essentially, authenticity derives from a difference. It's about revealing the quirks of your personality or brand. When you communicate your unique value proposition, you're building authenticity and therefore trust.

However, when authenticity was applied to interior design, it was not an alluring look. Mismatched furniture and the host's clutter could not seduce all travellers. Instead, they yearned for manufactured authenticity. Furniture that is visually merchandised to perfection. They wanted exposed brickwork, plant stands and neo-mid-century styling.

Unfortunately, when everyone is following the same trend, it becomes orthodox and a little bit boring! Back to the vanilla flavour. Authenticity is lost.

# BRAND PERSONALITY

*Activity*

—

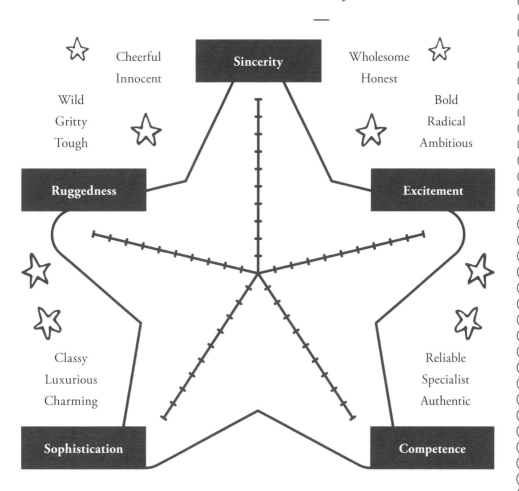

Mark a dot on each scale and join these up to create a star. The further the mark is from the centre, the higher the value. For example, a highly specialist brand would place a mark nearest the word 'Competence' on the respective scale.

Yes, it is crucial to give the people what they want but keep things fresh. And, as you can see, it's a real balancing act! Are you still unique? Yes? No? Think about it! It is OK to change your value proposition from time to time. Be like Madonna and reinvent yourself.

To create a complete and unique brand identity system with a strong value proposition, you need to consider: the brand as a product, the brand as a person, the brand as an organisation and the brand as a symbol. This model was adapted from David A. Aaker (2010) and it's our tried-and-tested method for creating a deep and authentic strategy.

## *4.1*  BRAND AS A PRODUCT

### CASE STUDY – LIGHT+NINE

Light+Nine, a US childrenswear brand, is one of our most treasured design partners. And – oh boy – do they care about the product! School books are heavy, right? Kids put so much strain on their growing backs because standard backpacks offer little support. That's why Light+Nine specialises in super lightweight backpacks. The founder designs with kids in mind and boasts an award-winning patented product range. The brand has surged ahead of the competition with major stockists like Neiman Marcus and Nordstrom, thanks to their innovative product design. Customers have the freedom of choice, so show them that you truly offer the best.

. . . . . . . . . . . . . . . . . .

Whenever we ask founders why their business is better than competitors, the usual answers are: "We're more advanced", "We're high quality" or "We offer the best value". These are attributes of the product (or service). A clear brand identity can help to communicate these benefits. However, we must offer a word of warning: if this was all we based our brands upon, there would be countless clone corporations. Product attributes are easy to copy — any confectionery brand can say "We're delicious!" Yet, no one wants to be a cookie-cutter, vanilla-flavoured brand! With more of us starting our own businesses, competition is fierce, so we need to combat this to give ourselves a fighting chance.

## 4.2 BRAND AS A PERSON

Your business is multi-layered, just like you. It has depth, personality and a genuine voice. Does your customer know this? You've got to express yourself! So next, consider your brand as a person. Sometimes it can help to think of a figure in the public eye for inspiration. Remember though, the brand as a person is not necessarily your customer. For example, when people use a law practice, they expect their solicitor to be professional and bursting with expertise. Yet, your customer may not necessarily show these traits themselves.

Social psychologist, J. Aaker (1997), identified 5 different dimensions of an authentic brand personality. These are:

1. Sincerity
2. Excitement
3. Competence
4. Sophistication
5. Ruggedness

How does your brand rate in each of these? Note this down to help steer your strategy. It may inspire a collection of words which describe your brand personality, such as: friendly, mischievous, supportive, forward-thinking and charismatic. These can always be handy to refer to when writing communications.

This personality will make your company feel more human and therefore, more likeable. Moreover, by personifying your organisation, you will instinctively know what will be "on-brand" when making essential decisions. Brand management will feel natural.

## 4.3 BRAND AS AN ORGANISATION

Great! Your brand has a personality but, to achieve a genuine voice, we need to develop it further. One way to create this voice is to consider the brand as an organisation. Brand associations which are driven by the organisation are less tangible than product or service attributes but play a strong role in supporting customer relationships.

What do we mean by this? It's your business' culture and values, the assets, the team, the programmes or initiatives and your visibility. These, when communicated, set the right expectations both internally and externally for a business. By adopting an organisational association, you are strengthening your value proposition, giving the customer another reason to buy. It gives your business a competitive edge (just as branding should do).

For example, The Body Shop is associated with being an environmentally-conscious organisation. By being a business that "gives back" and does the "right thing", they become increasingly likeable. It differentiates them from beauty brands that are solely focused on the value or product features. It increases trust and conveys their expertise in this area.

Think about what you truly stand for. Could one of the following associations work in your favour?

★ Innovator
★ Customer Carer
★ Local expert
★ Global expert
★ Environmentally-conscious
★ Community-orientated

For example, if your organisation is a "local expert", it makes sense to have local employees around locally-inspired imagery. Heritage will always stand in your favour as you become a keystone of the community. One brand revered by communities close to its origin is IRN-BRU. Although the brand has gained success further afield, it is still a local hero. It's known as Scotland's other national drink (whisky being the original). They use Scottish imagery to help connect with the audience at its roots. After all, there needs to be a trustworthy familiarity to bridge the gap between employees, candidates, investors and clients.

On the other hand, if you're a "global innovator", consider adopting diverse photography and using a forward-thinking tone of voice. You may have multiple locations across Earth to support your global image. To adapt to various cultures, you may need to adjust your communication from region to region. Many global organisations hire agents to act within each district. It's so important to have trustworthy ambassadors for your product or service that lives and breathes it every day.

The benefits of adopting one of these associations are bountiful. You can create a meaningful value proposition, gain a competitive edge, promote customer relationships based on feelings and it can provide product ranges with an "identity umbrella". It's good for your team too — they'll gain a sense of purpose and community to motivate them. By associating your brand with certain archetypes, customers can identify themselves within your brand. On a subconscious level, archetypes create a story which assumes far greater relevance and significance for customers.

## 4.4  BRAND AS A SYMBOL

Symbols within your brand identity can be used as metaphors to tell a richer story. The symbol is a vehicle of message.

Apple has adopted a famous symbol. It represents the apple that supposedly hit Isaac Newton on his head when discovered gravity. This harks back to Apple's first logo which featured the physicist himself. An individual who dared to think differently. The apple is also an iconic fruit and reflects the simplicity they aim to offer to the public.

A lot of businesses we have partnered with struggle to decide on a precise symbol with the pressure that it will become the everlasting "face of the company". They're aiming to create something simple, yet never seen before. However, there's no need to reinvent the wheel. Your brand is a living thing and should evolve. The symbol needn't be your forever-logo! It can simply act as a seal of approval or a graphic device. Get creative. Get started. Get confident.

Buttercrumble's symbol is a love heart — one of the most recognisable symbols to man. Again, it's simple and easily understood. It also doubles as a "B" for Buttercrumble. It immediately shows our audience that we are approachable and we care. When combined with the rest of our brand identity system, it takes on a life of its own. Don't be afraid to evoke emotion through your own brand's symbolism.

In short, your brand is most effective when you have different systems interacting with one another to create a whole. Combine the thinking of your brand as a: product, person, organisation and symbol for maximum impact. This mix creates a value proposition that's truly unique and difficult for competitors to imitate.

Finally, ask yourself, "what would the world be missing if my brand didn't exist?" If the answer is "nothing" then how can you expect customers to truly care? You need to nurture a uniqueness that your audience cannot replace. Don't be another "so what?"

^     *Light+Nine and their award-winning backpacks, photo by Amy Carson Photography*

*Chapter 5*

# CREDIBILITY

*Use your magic.*

---

## 5.1  YOUR EXPERTISE

Ten, twenty, thirty (or more) years of experience. It's something many collaborators claim. We respect the wisdom which follows from decades of practice. However, don't let it dishearten you if you're still a sapling. Experience ain't all it's cracked up to be!
Maybe we are biassed. At this moment, we are a young business and still learning every day. We cannot conjure up decades of experience, but we won't let this stop us from being taken seriously. In fact, we can use it to our advantage.

The Walt Disney Company has been known to introduce a "naive expert" to creative, development discussions (Business Centre, 2018). These ingenious people have little knowledge on the topic of interest, so are able to encourage bilateral thinking. They ask the stupid questions you are too afraid to ask. They are able to suggest crazy ideas from their cluelessness. This courage is a catalyst for innovation. Innovation helps an organisation continuously improve their offerings.

This shortage of experience means you may be fearless in your decision making. The lack of "baggage" means you're agile. In turn, you are able to achieve more, instead of panicking about past occurrences. After all, ignorance is bliss and you simply cannot be troubled by what is unknown. Instead, your spirit shines through. This youthful enthusiasm is infectious, so use it before you lose it.

In time, this enthusiasm turns to wisdom. At that point, the tables have turned. You can now broadcast your experience to your heart's content. Although, if you do hear yourself boasting "I have twenty years experience", pause for a moment–– Remember you were once a naive expert too.

The advantage of experience is increased credibility. It's the quality of being trusted and dependable. After all, you've been refining your craft for many years — you know your onions. It's important to nurture your credibility because the business landscape is saturated and innovative brands are being born left, right and centre. You are watching the competition with an eagle eye, jumping on band-wagons, and showing your customers you can do anything!

If you still find you're struggling to drum up custom, it might not be price-related or your lack of diversity. The reason could lie in your lack of distinction. You now have the credibility, but you're not displaying it properly.

When you become a generalist, you're competing with thousands of other generalists. If you can identify your magic, you can cut-out the competition. If you position your brand as an expert, you become the go-to destination for your customers. You're the logical choice as you offer what they want. As a result, they know they're in safe hands and can expect a return on their investment.

**Remember:** if you're trying to speak to everyone, you're speaking to no one!

Better yet, YOU can expect a return on your self-investment. By positioning yourself as an expert there is less need to engage in negotiations and bartering. Less is more. You avoid being a busy fool (working hard for a pittance) by valuing your work properly. You are delivering absolute gold dust to your customers and their investment should reflect this.

"But how do I find my expertise?" We hear you cry! Experience does help. Yet, there are many ways you could spot a niche within your business. This could be through your approach to customer service, process, style, or your innovative product. Defining your value proposition and expertise is not an easy task. You need to get right down to the nitty-gritty and address your customer's pain points as well as acknowledging your own magic. As ABBA (and Alan Partridge) once said it's "knowing me, knowing you. Aha".

When we launched the business officially back in January 2017, we were a pair of fresh-faced twenty-two-year-olds, straight out of University. What did we know about business? Entrepreneurship didn't run in the family, we had no business qualifications, and we'd barely dipped our toes in the creative industry.

We knew we were naive and inexperienced but we knew we had the gumption to succeed. Our motto was "Fake it 'til you make it and learn along the way"! We put the hours in to ensure we were as equipped as possible to tackle the business-world. By having this self-awareness, we could foresee any doubts potential clients might have regarding our potential.

It was essential that we communicated our expertise. We both felt confident to deliver the design needs of our clients. Yes, we had only just completed our degrees in graphic and communication design but we'd been designing since we could pick up a pencil. We were sharing our work online in 2008 when we began to complete art-trades and small commissions. Before starting Buttercrumble, we had nine years of experience answering briefs and many more just nurturing our imaginations.

Of course, the degrees are powerful tools in our repertoire. If you receive accreditation from one of the globally-leading universities, don't be afraid to flaunt it, you earned it! We regularly refer to our education when delivering talks and workshops to prove we've completed training and know our stuff. What we deliver isn't just fluffy pictures, we have the design knowledge and research skills to bolster any visual creations. I imagine we'll need to refer to this less as we grow, take on new challenges, and receive different credentials. For the time being, it's an achievement we're proud of and to celebrate this only brings us favours.

This said, we still knew it was not enough to work with bigger companies. Business owners need to know they're in a trusted pair of hands, executives need to know they won't have egg on their face. We all want to appear competent and essential to our teams. Why would any business take a risk on a pair of new graduates? We knew we had to clearly demonstrate we could deliver the goods through past experience.

We worked hard to curate a portfolio to be proud of. We ensured any personal projects answered the brief (it doesn't matter if it's fictitious), provided a solution and celebrated our creativity. We were honing our style to give clear expectations to potential clients. As soon as we completed a "real" brief for a "real" client, we would replace one of our personal projects with some fully-fledged experience. If you take this approach, you may find your portfolio becomes mismatched and your style becomes diluted, but keep the faith. This was a crucial activity for us as we were able to spot patterns and trends emerging in our projects. As a result, we could evaluate and refine our portfolio further, and distil it to its finest form. We now know that it's best to follow the motto "quality over quantity", it is difficult to curate just a handful of case-studies which embody your offering, but it's advantageous when done right. This careful curation of offerings applies to all businesses.

Sure, you can talk-the-talk but can you walk-the-walk? You need to prove you can deliver with ease, in-budget, and on-time? Testimonials are a great tool to have in your repertoire and these can be applied across so many business models. Customers want to know you've been tried-and-tested and you've delivered the results to their friends, family, peers and neighbours. You are reducing the amount of potential risk and customers will feel more compelled to buy.

To ask for a testimonial can feel a little awkward and vulnerable, but the benefits outweigh those negative feelings. We ask for general feedback on our projects and avoid leading questions. It's important that your customers/clients feel valued and listened to. Try asking questions like:

- ⭐ What was your favourite part of your experience and why?
- ⭐ If you were to recommend our brand to a friend, what would you say?
- ⭐ Did the product/service meet your expectations?
- ⭐ What would have made your experience with us better?
- ⭐ Were we able to satisfy your needs?

Testimonials and practical evidence can demonstrate your expertise. If you want to take this to the next level, show you're a thought-leader and not just a skilled disciple, you can hold talks. Speaking opportunities hold gravitas because it shows you have the confidence to share your knowledge — publicly — with an audience. Public speaking can be daunting but it sure does deliver the wow-factor.

## ABIGAIL'S REFLECTION

66 One of our first "official" talks was at Leeds College of Art (now Leeds Arts University) in February 2017. This was merely a month after launching the business but it just proves that even infants can parade their expertise. Consider who would be interested in your story to improve your chances of being selected for a gig. Many of our talks have been to students at the different educational institutes within Leeds because we can relate to their needs. Our student days are still in-reach, and this is when we can use youth to our advantage. This experience is fantastic and we're keen advocates for creative education, however, those talks do not reach our customers directly.

The first talk we delivered outside of Leeds was in July 2017 at the Business Design Centre, London. It was our big chance to speak to customers in an industry setting — Bubble London. Bubble London is a respected, premium kidswear and lifestyle brands trade show. It was an honour to attend and be seen amongst some of the biggest names in the childrenswear industry. It gave us the opportunity to chat with global brands and boutique independents, as well as seeing the big city.

Over two days, we created a brand activation where we illustrated portraits of visitors. This gave us the perfect opportunity to speak to business owners and trade visitors. And — of course — we performed our branding seminar.

It was nerve-racking as our voices were projected to the whole centre, making it our biggest audience to date (at the time). Plus, it never helps your confidence when there are audio problems, nonetheless it was great to share the value of visuals with everyone. We presented ways to grow your fan base through branding, imparting insider knowledge on how to convert strangers to ambassadors through clever tactics, as well as what makes a likeable business. I felt our expertise resonated with our audience as — after the seminar — we were approached by a number of businesses. Although no direct sales were generated, it gave us an extra feather in our cap and the confidence to continue.

. . . . . . . . . . . . . . . . . .

In September 2019 we returned to London as panellists, in another prestigious venue, at Bonhams Auctioneers. Again, this demonstrated the importance of sharing your expertise with the right audience. We spoke to a room of key decision-makers within the creative industry about our experience of the National Saturday Club.

The National Saturday Club was inspired by British art schools between the late 1940s and 1970s. Many schools opened their doors on Saturdays to inspire young people and spark creative spirits. The Club's co-founders, Sir John and Lady Frances Sorrell, both started their professional journeys by attending these Saturday art classes. After ten years of developing pioneering educational programmes, the Foundation launched the first National Art & Design Saturday Club in 2009.

We participated in the club back in 2010 and 2011. It changed our outlook on creative careers, so we were delighted to encourage others to embrace the arts. Our story touched some of the industry-experts watching and we received mentoring opportunities, as well as strengthening our relationship with the Sorrells. We used the time to express our expertise, passion, and business strengths whilst thanking the Club for their support during our education. This helped us to strike a balance and communicate our authenticity.

If you're nervous about performing to a crowd, you can hold a more intimate workshop where participants are involved. This takes some of the attention away from you and projects it onto your audience, it also helps to make them feel engaged and involved. We have held a number of workshops to a variety of audiences from young children to industry

# PERSONAL VALUES

*Activity*

—

What values matter to you? Write them under the three different categories below.

| Life | Business | Relationships |
|------|----------|---------------|
| • *Self-development* | • *Profitability* | • *Honesty* |
| • *Integrity* | • *Innovation* | • *Empathy* |
| • *Beauty* | • *Teamwork* | • *Respect* |

Select your three top values from each category above:

1. ..................    1. ..................    1. ..................

2. ..................    2. ..................    2. ..................

3. ..................    3. ..................    3. ..................

experts and it's a fantastic networking opportunity. It also provides you with an insight into our audience's thoughts and beliefs. If you can stay in-touch and connected with your customers, you are more likely to resonate with them.

The practice of public relations is important when building credibility as you can take advantage of trusted intermediaries. Make strategic alliances with your PR outlets and you can communicate to specific audiences. We have appeared on a number of creative blogs, in industry magazines, local and national newspapers. To appear in a publication holds a lot of weight for consumers as the media is still seen as a trusted news source (despite criticism). We always jump at the opportunity to leverage the media, it voices our expertise to new and broader audiences, who we may not reach through our own marketing.

Furthermore, is your product or service news-worthy? We've had the pleasure of working on some quirky projects which made great stories. Back in 2017, Leeds Dock underwent exciting regeneration bringing many visitors and residents back to the area. We worked closely with Leeds Dock, Allied London and The Royal Armouries to create a giant Snakes and Ladders board (with a mediaeval twist) on the plaza outside the Armouries.

We were involved with the project from start-to-finish… Despite being a fledgling business, we attended meetings with Allied London to determine the creative concept for the project, used Adobe Illustrator to create the visuals, and finally liaised with the print suppliers to ensure the illustrations were art-worked correctly. The illustrations were printed on vinyl and then arranged on the plaza measuring over 20m wide by the supplier.

We added extra touches of interactivity to make the game even more engaging. This includes a range of fun facts for knights and knightesses to ponder along the way and a castle that can be coloured in using chalks. It was a joy to see families interacting with the game over the Easter season.

## CHLOE'S REFLECTION

❝ The project received press coverage through Made in Leeds and The Yorkshire Post but we had to work fast to meet the journalist's deadlines. In the early months of this project, Abigail was supporting in-house at a digital marketing agency, I worked on remote projects in the meantime. At 9:00 am, the phone rang, it was a PR specialist working with Leeds Dock. She explained that Made in Leeds, the local television station, were interested in covering the story. "Can you be at the Royal Armouries at 10:30 am for an interview?" Well, I lived a twenty-minute drive from the Armouries so it didn't leave much shuffle-room! I agreed to the interview and made a mad dash to the car. If you're a freelancer at home, do not work in your pyjamas! You never know when you might have a chance encounter. Dress up, show up and never give up. Be ready to strike at the perfect occasion. Despite the fluster, nerves, and lack of preparation, the interview was a big success. People recall the project and it introduced us to a wider local audience.

Credibility becomes a self-feeding loop for your brand. People trust you, so they pay attention to your brand. If your brand is thoughtfully designed, then you improve memorability. Strong brand recall can encourage long-term success for your organisation. Be consistently iconic.

Often, we set up a business because we feel we can offer something different, something better and something special. You know your offering is special, otherwise you would never go through the toil of establishing a new company — it's hard work! However, so many new businesses don't infuse this enthusiasm into their visual identity. They don't communicate their specialness. There's no one that knows your extraordinary business like you do. So spread your passion and share your story. Your organisation can create a legacy.

Don't forget to acknowledge your achievements to ensure your success is visible. It creates a brand image of competence and reliability, which reassures customers. If you're confident, customers will be too. They also feel safe when they know other consumers have invested in the brand.

## 5.2   YOUR PERSONAL BRAND

Brands are relevant to everyone. Even though we usually associate it with companies, we all have individual personal brands too. How do you manage people's expectations of you? After all, we all know the importance of first impressions and we all have the power to influence these.

By considering your own personal brand, you can stand out from the crowd, attract more opportunities and the right people who will support your goals. But, how do you develop a personal brand? Isn't it deeply ingrained in our identities?

Your personal brand should feel like a natural reflection of you. You can develop and define your own personal brand by considering your purpose. To find your purpose, you need to ask yourself three questions:

1.  What are you passionate about?
2.  What are you good at?
3.  What does the world need?

This will give a well-rounded vision of your purpose. If you're stuck or would like to take this activity to the next level, consider where you'd like to be in five or ten years time. Your personal brand can be the vehicle to take you there.

You — as an individual — may differ from your business' personality. If there's a tension between your personal values and business values, it can make business decisions challenging. Create clarity for yourself by writing down three titles: "life", "business", and "relationships". Under each title, list your relevant values.

It can be overwhelming if you have more than five values per category, so begin to prioritise and rate each one in order of importance. Narrow down your list to three core values per category. The example's values are different, but harmonious. This kind of regular self-reflection tunes your life compass and makes important decisions so much easier. You'll feel less tension and will become at ease when you live by your true values.

Ensure this activity is a meaningful use of your time. Don't write down values because you think they make you look good and don't be influenced by others. Personal brands work best when they're authentic. Believe us — nothing rings more alarm bells than a phoney. We've met "personal brands" who swear they believe in integrity and helping others, but only when it helps them. That's why, when we deliver talks, we insist that audiences reach out to us. We provide paid student placements, mentor younger businesses, and have coffee dates with under-served talent.

It's shocking how many experts can talk the talk, but don't walk the walk. Perhaps it's our industry — an industry designed to sell — it attracts the best schmoozers and snake charmers.

Personal branding was our guiding star and its positive magic helped us take the leap into full-time self-employment! It brightened our path through university where we were joined by a few wise men (our supervisors). They shared the wisdom of the star and we learned how a personal brand can complement your business brand and — combined — build success and notoriety.

We received the most influential guidance when we sat down with our university tutor to discuss industry experience and career paths — three years before we took our business leap of faith — and he referred us to the careers centre at our university. From there, we applied for an enterprise scholarship, and were selected for an interview.

We prepared meticulously for our "Dragons' Den" business pitch, attending all the support workshops, tours and seminars we could, as the thought of talking to a panel of judges gave us "the willies". It can be scary to talk about your idea out loud — it makes it oh-so-real — what if it fails?

One of the judges took us on a tour of the enterprise hub at the University and (thank goodness) he recognised our passion. He kindly offered to coach us through the looming pitch and we lapped up the support… We're really glad we did.

He gave us a piece of advice that we still use to this day — "use your smile". This is funny because, throughout periods of our childhood and teenage years, our smiles felt like a curse. Put simply, we're not lacking in the tooth department and orthodontists were our friends. Collectively, we had twelve of our teeth removed, wore braces for seven years, and were nicknamed "Jaws" at one point. But — like in the tale of The Ugly Duckling — two smiling swans emerged. We now smile at all given opportunities and boy did we smile through that interview.

Today, we regularly bump into the coach who crowned us the "happiest women in business" and we wear this as our personal brand. We convey a positive and uplifting energy and attract like-minded folk to our business. Smiles make the designs and our designs make you smile.

Once you have your personal brand, don't be afraid to push it one step further. If you think it's too much, it's probably just right. If you can evoke an emotional reaction, when you walk into a room, you'll be remembered.

This is so important as a business owner, because you want to be the first person that springs into your audience's mind when they need your product/service.

**Here are three quick hacks to level up your personal brand:**

1. If you like colour, don't be afraid to embrace it in your wardrobe! Wear a bright colour palette religiously to be recognised, photographed, and talked about.
2. Do you wear prescription glasses? Try unusual frames — they can be oversized, colourful, or even asymmetric. Spectacles can be a game-changing accessory and a fun talking point.
3. Get a haircut. Find a good hair stylist and colourist who can work with you to define your individual style and personal brand. Hair is a major form of self-expression so embrace what you have (or don't have — baldness is a super power).

**What's unique about you and how can you use it as part of your personal brand?**

## 5.3   YOUR ENTREPRENEURIAL SELF

We are advocates for an authentic personal brand, however, everyone has foibles to be conscious of. Your "true self" might be sitting in front of the television in your underwear and a fluffy dressing gown, but that's not the self you'd bring to a corporate business meeting. Everyone has an "on-stage" and "off-stage" personality and your personal brand needs to take on-stage, centre-stage.

Personal brands can come and go, but your values are constant. Bizz-bosses value entrepreneurship and they're fully committed to the mindset. Authentic business owners are not measured by their Girl Boss sign or signature haircut. They are measured by their entrepreneurial spirit and, if you can't foster this, you will not survive. Business is hard.

You are the greatest project you will ever work on.

## CHLOE'S REFLECTION

❝ I grew up in a town with very little creative industry. Moreover, my family is employed in non-creative, working class roles. Despite this, they have always supported my sisters and I in our pursuit for creativity… with an air of caution.

"If you want this, you've got to work hard at it".

We've all taken this wisdom on-board and we're grateful for it. In 2016, Abigail and I graduated from the University of Leeds. With a degree in graphic and communication design, and a prestigious scholarship award under our belts, we were able to kick-start our business, Buttercrumble.

We are proud to be the first in our family, for generations, to graduate from university. I'm also super proud to see my youngest sister do the same, and she is (at the time of writing) studying in Newcastle.

As I said, our family is not from a business background, but they inadvertently instilled an entrepreneurial spirit in us. Passion and hard-work are integral to the mindset.

· · · · · · · · · · · · · · · · · ·

The entrepreneurial mindset is similar to the "growth mindset" coined by leading psychologist, Dr Carol Dweck, and challenges perceptions of ingrained potential (2017). You are not simply born good or bad at sports, or music, or business. The growth mindset promotes learning as people who adopt it believe their abilities can improve with effort and discipline; they persevere when faced with challenges!

On the other end of the spectrum is a "fixed mindset" — a dangerous frame of mind for business people. If you believe your abilities are innate, you have a fixed mindset. What's more, this mindset is as comfortable as it is dangerous. To be good or bad at something is often taken as a person's identity, "oh, I'm naturally flexible", or "I've never been good at maths" is a comfort blanket of acceptance. People don't want to deviate from the accepted image of themselves. This prevents many from adopting a growth mindset; it costs them time, energy, and money.

However, you've got to take the steps to the top. A growth mindset can cultivate true entrepreneurial spirit. With each step, you will muster the grit and determination you need to succeed in business.

It's not easy to maintain a growth mindset if (like so many busy people) you're lacking headspace. Entrepreneurs must make space for their health and wellbeing. It's something we prioritise as "the happiest women in business" but we're no strangers to sadness. We're not promoting toxic positivity — darkness is inevitable — we're promoting bounce-back-ability!

How do you bounce back quicker and stronger? You need to surround yourself with positive influences and people who will uplift and inspire you. As twins, we're fortunate to have a built-in support network. We've been through the majority of our life experiences together — the good, the bad, and the ugly — so we're empathetic. Join clubs or societies to cultivate your own support network. Mindset is contagious.

This said, we can't rely on others alone and strength must also come from within. We're believers in "fake it until you make it". At first, it might feel cringe-worthy to look at your reflection and say "you got this", but you need to practise positive self-talk and self-care. We all know that a balanced diet and regular physical activity are key to a healthy lifestyle, but mental wellbeing can be underplayed. Your mind needs continuous care and attention.

Resilience can be built through self-awareness. Dedicate time to introspection and, through journalling or meditation, you can reflect on your actions and emotions. A written record enables entrepreneurs to look back at positive patterns and, ensuing, align their values and goals to their business. When your business makes you feel good, you become a magnet for success.

You become resilient when you learn to accept yourself and your imperfections. Expect failure, but expect recovery too. At the end of the day, we're all human beings who get things wrong, but you have survived your worst days yet. You will bounce back. We've found this kind of attitude — to remember life's rich tapestry — takes the edge off the dark times. We know misfortune, but it gives us the perspective to appreciate the good times.

And, did we mention how helpful a sense of humour can be? Life is short so we might as well enjoy ourselves. We've tackled many stressful business challenges while creased up with laughter. Once we were building our exhibit at a prestigious trade event, we'd spent big bucks, our peers were watching (judging), and we were hauling furniture about. We were desperately trying to affix signage, in wintry temperatures, while wrapped up like Arctic explorers. We had forgotten our drill and thought it would be a good idea to hammer a nail into a hefty wall with no muscle power. It was a disaster, but what could we do? We laughed. Then we used our happy charms to make friends and get free assistance.

A negative attitude won't get you half as far. You got this!!!

**How to cultivate your entrepreneurial self?**

Give the negative voice a name. You know the voice that says, "you can't do that", "give up", or "you've never been any good"? That voice is usually formed in childhood, but you're now a grown and capable adult. You can achieve anything you set your mind to! Detach the voice from your ego by naming that negative Nellie. You take the wind out of those sails when you can say, "oh, shut up, [insert name here]".

Don't be hard on yourself. Be honest, when was the last time you learned something new? They say you can't teach an old dog new tricks, because it takes time and effort to learn a new skill. We get used to our own ways of doing things. So… jubilate when you commit to those language lessons and don't despair when you're the slowest in swimming class! We don't laugh at babies when they're learning to walk, we hold their hands, and cheer words of encouragement. Be kind to yourself.

Don't let failure define you. It seems so irrational to label ourselves as "failures" when it is just a part of everyday life. As soon as you can accept mistakes as a normal part of life and our shared human experience, you destroy its power. We all fail, but it teaches us humility, resourcefulness, and perspective. Failure is the "first (second, or third…) attempt in learning"! It doesn't need to define you.

Turn a negative into a positive. Failure can be hugely motivating. If something goes wrong, let it spur you on! Sometimes we receive a "no" to our proposals, but we turn this into a positive. It's not "no, never", it's a "no, not yet". You're yet to succeed!

## 5.4   A WOMAN'S POWER

For centuries, men were promoted as the best business leaders and a woman's place was in the kitchen. Even during the arts and crafts movement of the 19th and 20th century, when feminine past-times were commercialised, men took centre-stage. Female artisans were not as widely recognised as names like William Morris or John Ruskin. History repeated itself with the iconic Bauhaus movement of the early 20th century when many talented women failed to receive the same accolades as their male classmates.

This bias still exists today. In women's magazines, business is often pitched as a flexible side-hustle that can be moulded around childcare duties. The culture around women in business can be pretty toxic. This is evident with The Wing controversy. Senior journalist, Susannah Butter, describes how the "feminist utopia" became subject to complaints of misgendering and racism (2020). Obviously these kinds of behaviours cannot be condoned, but it's interesting to see how quickly the media rushes to cancel female-founded companies.

WeWork, an office startup, is also clouded in controversy. There have been various documented claims of sexual harassment, employment crime, and race discrimination. However, despite this, the male-owned company has been glamorised. In 2021, AppleTV announced a new show following the rise and fall of the organisation in a spectacular and star-studded fashion.

Women have historically been victims of witch-hunts for all matters — too rich, too poor, too clever — and this needs to stop. If we are to truly empower women, we need to support all women and marginalised groups.

We feel female leadership, in particular, is important within a creative business. There is increasing evidence that a diverse workforce produces more effective solutions. On the strength of diversity, fresh perspectives can highlight information which homogeneous groups may overlook. A number of thought-leaders including Harvard Business Review (2021) are advocates for women-led organisations. They believe women are more likely to "innovate" and "demonstrate learning agility" which are key requirements when producing new creative solutions for clients.

In 2019, the UK Treasury commissioned Alison Rose (former CEO of NatWest) to complete an independent review of female entrepreneurship. The study uncovered the untapped potential of businesswomen to the tune of "around £250 billion". This is if women "chose to start and scale businesses at the same rate as men" (Rose, 2019, p.18).

The report describes how women are typically more cautious than men and this prevents them from taking the leap. Don't let your fear hold you back, harness this energy, as it will help you to make decisions. By acknowledging the risks of business, you can forge a stronger path forward.

In addition, it's argued that women are less confident in their entrepreneurial abilities than men. The study found that its female participants often downplayed their own successes whilst crediting others. Although this is proof of a woman's supportive nature, it's a shame we cannot support ourselves! Whilst promoting others, don't forget to take a moment to recognise your own achievements.

We've had the pleasure of working with many amazing business women over the years. Harness your unique power, and build a diverse team, for a wiser and more creative organisation.

## 5.5   SUPPORTING OTHERS

When running a business we believe karma is more important than ever. What you put out in the world can come back to you in unexpected ways, we have certainly found this to be the case. Whether it's friends, family, colleagues, aspiring entrepreneurs, or even a passing stranger — we could all benefit from helping hand.

### CHLOE'S REFLECTION

❝ We are increasingly approached by students for help and advice. I must admit I've felt a bit uneasy giving advice to someone only a few years my junior. We are often asked how we started our business (fresh out of university). We tell them we've been working up to this present moment all our life, so it's difficult to consider all the things which came before. We think it's important to think of small achievable goals, from gaining valuable industry experience to building a long-term relationship with a client. Was it always our intention to start Buttercrumble? No. Was it an overnight success? No. It was a case of slowly, slowly, catchy monkey!

I remember hearing an analogy about a tomato plant; I think it can teach us a lot about personal and business growth. We buy the plant with the intention of harvesting ripe, juicy, tomatoes. We don't expect to plonk a few seeds in the ground and eat the plump fruits the next day. We must sew the seeds thoughtfully, ensure they are bathed in sunlight, watered, and the soil stays healthy. We weed out any stray plants or pests, we support the stem as it grows taller, until, eventually we are rewarded for our patience. We do not criticise or chastise that little plant but we might whisper words of gentle encouragement. You know what… we are not dissimilar from that little tomato plant. We all need support!

There's no such thing as an overnight success. As an outsider, it can seem like the success of many businesses was almost instant because they already have it all under control. Yet, the journey to get there was challenging and gruelling. We collect rejections every week. However, for every "no thanks" received, we know we're one step closer to a "yes please". You have to be consistently persistent over time. We celebrate the successes and not the failures, so these hardships never receive publicity. Patience and determination are key tools in your arsenal.

· · · · · · · · · · · · · · · · · · ·

Like many businesses, we sometimes feel squeezed under time pressures. It can be difficult to support and give-back to others. We do believe, though, that giving-back is a win-win situation, so why not make time? It can fit into your corporate social responsibilities (CSR) or even marketing strategy. In fact, you can leverage the reach and expertise of larger organisations, related to the interests of you, your industry or customers. By forming these partnerships, you can make a larger impact and reach the right audience whom you'd like to support. These organisations often have existing processes in place for partnership programmes, so they are ready and waiting for your collaboration!

At Buttercrumble, we've given back to many of the institutes and organisations who have supported us. For example, we have hosted free consultancy sessions, given presentations and delivered workshops whilst partnering with the Business & IP Centre (The British Library), IPSE, University of Leeds and the National Saturday Club.

These sorts of connections are called "brand partnerships". The best partnerships occur when both organisations have a synergy. Like all sustainable relationships, it needs to be harmonious with shared values and interests. It's also important to note whether they have a relevant audience who are going to benefit from you and your story. Usually, if you share values, you will share a similar audience. They go hand-in-hand.

By employing brand partnerships, we found we were able to accomplish three important activities:

**Re-engaging Our Audience**
When partnering with a new organisation, you are able to promote something different. It revitalises your communication and livens your audience up. The sight of a familiar identity aligned with another familiar identity always sparks the attention.

**Connect to a New Audience**

All of the organisations we have partnered with have promoted Buttercrumble. Whether it be social media posts, press releases or even photography shoots! These exciting opportunities have spread Buttercrumble to new audiences who may never have experienced us otherwise. Moreover, the partner brand acts as an endorser for your own organisation. When they back your brand, their audience are likely to back you too.

**Alter Perceptions**

When setting-up the business, it took a while to feel we were being taken seriously. A lot of people shrug start-ups off because of their lack of experience or dependability. However, the championship of a larger organisation can catapult you to a new level of credibility. Once we told people we had partnered with the likes of The British Library, they began to listen more.

How can you achieve this? Make staying-in-touch a habit and you'll be surprised at the amount of opportunities fly your way. Brand partnerships are built from relationships and these need to be nurtured over time. Our objectives for staying connected are: link-up on LinkedIn, follow their tweets and send biannual emails. Be regular and consistent to build genuine trust. A little bit of effort can go a long way to stay in the right people's minds.

*Chapter 6*

# RELATIONSHIPS

*Your network is your net worth.*

———————

Relationships play a huge role in branding. Ultimately, it's not just about selling a product — it's selling a belief. This is crucial, especially within the workplace. You can nurture faith and friendships when you connect emotionally with your team, stakeholders and clients. It's important to create a personality for your organisation and brand. This temperament and style is more effective at communicating your organisation's benefits than directly stating such benefits exist 24/7. It also enhances the likeability and authenticity of your business as a whole.

Yet, behind every brand, there is a real person. As a business owner or brand guardian, it's important you learn to be a well-rounded individual first. If you're unable to interact with others, it's going to be difficult to drive your company (and brand) forward. Empathy is going to allow you to connect with your audience and stakeholders. This builds stronger relationships and keeps your business alive. Communication is key and branding becomes a part of this.

This chapter explains in more detail how branding can influence your team, suppliers and clients and vice versa. After all, it takes two to tango!

## CHLOE'S REFLECTION

❝ The COVID-19 Crisis. It's March 2020, day three of UK isolation and a week has passed since Buttercrumble enforced home-working.

It's been fascinating to see the virus response ripple throughout the globe to our little corner of Yorkshire. In my opinion, some attitudes have been frustrating… stock-piling, theft, and gloomy outlooks have all surfaced. I think it's nature's way of wheedling out the weak from the brave.

Of course, as a business, we may need to make serious cut-backs. I am torn between my personal conscience and business sense. It's been a challenge to meet the financial success we so desired this year due to the increase in overheads, and now, the COVID-19.

I found it amusing when a connection of ours said "now is not the time for a hard sell". Isn't it the perfect time? I have felt a real shift in our working energy and attitude, we're back to the survival mode of our startup days. These are the tools to help us weather the storm. I say thank goodness that we are a twin-team and I know we can stay united.

I believe these situations are sent to us as opportunities and people often miss them because they're disguised as hard work. People's needs are changing and they yearn for engagement and connectivity — how can we deliver the right solution? Creativity is key to innovation and in times of crisis, new developments will arise.

The world is still turning and we are still pitching for work and delivering proposals during the crisis. After all, everyone's best interest is to push through and return to normal. I think the businesses who have the vision to deliver the biggest push, are the ones who have always stayed true to their values. We can appreciate how our work at Buttercrumble is more important than ever, we are here to create designs which make us smile, our clients smile and, in turn, make their customers smile too. Don't we all need that beautiful relief in these dark times? By keeping a positive mindset, we've not had to question our direction too much.

The COVID-19 outbreak has taught me the importance of relationships in business and personal life. In these moments of crisis, I think you discover who your real friends are.

It has been a joy to see people rally around and it makes you realise you should never fear to ask for help. I don't think any of this would be possible if we hadn't cultivated a community before the mess. It's so important to see community-building as a constant act of love. We should be gracious and grateful to our supporters and uplifters. People connect to authenticity and vulnerability — it takes time to create this.

Over the last week, I've been able to pick-up the phone to so many people. Everyone is having a hard time and we all can share support. From ourselves to clients, suppliers and the wider team — we are a community.

. . . . . . . . . . . . . . . . . .

## 6.1   YOUR TEAM

A job is no longer for life, as the workforce becomes more discerning. We all want our work to work well for us! Not just the other way around. For many, your occupation is a form of self-expression — it is a part of who you are. This is why a strong physical brand identity can recruit the perfect team for your workplace. It makes sense to cultivate a sense of branding within the workplace.

Moreover, skills can be taught, but values aren't quite the same. You simply can't force your brand values upon people, if they don't align with their own. A physical brand signposts what values you believe in, which then attracts a like-minded community.

Overall, the team is impacting on your audience's brand perceptions, as team members are usually touch-points in the customer journey. As well as driving the vision forward, your team are representatives for the brand. They should be the organisation's biggest ambassadors, so it's best to make sure everyone is on board with the organisation's missions and values.

Physical branding in the workplace has become a trend with the rise of the gig economy and flexible working. The option of climbing the career ladder is no longer linear. It's no longer just about the money! People want employment that suits their lifestyle, values and needs and will be picky in order to gain this. Organisations are taking bold steps in building a brand to cultivate loyalty and retain talent.

The best brands allow people to be themselves within a community. They can work as fashion statements. It links back to self-expression. This is why it's so important that your branding starts from the inside (for your team) and works outwards (to clients). It is crucial everyone is representing or supporting the business in the best possible way. This can be achieved when branding starts at the company's core.

If your brand is cohesive, it can help shape your organisation's values and approach as the team can feel fully invested in the business' mission. It becomes a shining example for your team to embrace and follow. If employees don't understand your brand, they lack direction and ultimately fail as ambassadors for the business. It can be worth asking employees "do you know what the brand stands for? What is our vision and how do you share it?" From this, you can discover whether the team feels an emotional connection and if they truly care. A strong brand prompts speedy responses. If there is hesitation and uncertainty, it may signal the need for clearer messaging.

Your team can measure their actions on the organisation's brand values, if they are clear. At Buttercrumble, "collaboration" is one of our core values. By communicating this, the team knows that clients expect this sense of community. Therefore, they are more likely to express this value in the work they do. Everyone is invested in the brand and its meaning so they are motivated to uphold these values. They're committed to making things happen because of the additional direction provided and hopefully feel proud to be withholding such positive values. If your brand has no direction, the team may feel misguided and confused about priorities.

Moreover, you can paint your visual brand until the cows come home, but unless your employees are communicating the right message, all your design-work can come undone. Customers will interact with your brand through your employees and their actions and attitudes become central to the delivery of your intentions. Do they meet the expectations you have set through your logo and colour scheme? Do they meet your promises? As a brand-owner, you can control the overall look and feel of your brand, but human interaction is unpredictable. This can be a brand's downfall.

This is why it's so important that your branding starts from the inside and works outwards. After all, you have to have trustworthy ambassadors for your product that lives and breathes it every day. Otherwise, how do you expect customers to truly connect? The team bridges the gap between consumer and product, by providing a human touch. It is crucial everyone is representing the business in the best possible way — you are your own biggest cheerleaders. This can be achieved when branding starts at the company's core.

Visual reminders are a great way to express your brand values to the team. Ensure you are presenting the identity across your online collaboration tools. Your branding can be carried across your emails, project management systems, office decor and staff room.

IKEA is a great example of using branding to create a strong company culture and instantly recognisable brand. Their stores visually feature their key brand values such as "togetherness" and "caring for the planet". Internally, they promote two-way conversations across their intranet. This results in staff feeling listened to and part of the team. Their internal communications are often location-specific to ensure they cultivate a personable brand that really speaks to the team. Therefore, members are engaged! Don't just take our word for it though, Glassdoor (2019) rated IKEA #16 for best places to work (in the UK).

By using internal branding, you can help to shape employees' behaviour is largely based on the assumption that when employees understand and are committed to the brand values inherent in the brand promise, they will perform in ways that live up to customers' brand expectations. To ensure your team can deliver the brand promise, the business needs to foster their employees' brand understanding through proper training, systems and technology.

## CHLOE'S REFLECTION

**"** This clear internal communication takes me back to my college work at McDonald's. Everyone knows, no matter where you are in the world, you know what you're going to get at McDonald's. That familiarity fills you with a warm sense of safety. How do they master consistency? Everything is systematised and communicated visually. Diagrams fill the employee areas of the restaurant, the handbook is a bible, and the training is ongoing. They don't leave their food up to chance — everything is defined down to the specific ingredients and exact placement. They don't leave their service up to chance — servers memorise scripts and are timed on their delivery. They don't leave restaurant experience up to chance — it is constantly reviewed and monitored. They connect the performance of their workforce through internal brand communication. Despite systems, you still feel like an integral part of the big picture. They express your value through personal touches and a rewards system.

Internal communications has been one of the biggest battles at Buttercrumble as we've found it hard to accept that few others will love the business as much as we do. I dislike the phrase "your business is your baby" but I suppose it is in that sense. We've implemented the knowledge and the systems.

· · · · · · · · · · · · · · · · · ·

It's vital you cultivate a strong culture of communication in order to bolster your team's engagement. You can achieve this by adopting a multi-touch approach. By using multiple communication channels — such as newsletters, social media, and letters — you increase the chances that everyone in the organisation will receive your message.

With more people working remotely, instant messaging (IM) can be a valuable communication channel. IM tools allow you to reach out to your team instantaneously, allowing you to boost collaboration and transparency.

Newsletters (digital or physical) are an effective form of internal communication as they can be planned, structured, and branded. A carefully crafted newsletter allows you to get your voice heard whilst involving and informing your employees. Avoid appearing unreliable and scatty through impromptu communication, use consistent messaging to demonstrate the genuine consideration you give your business.

We're strong believers that communication is a two-way street. You won't learn anything new by broadcasting messages with no real dialogue. Your audience has a voice too so empower your team to be open with their ideas and feedback.

Create an organised feedback system through polls or surveys and receive anonymous suggestions. Be approachable by promoting an open door policy. Your team should be able to raise any questions or challenges.

## 6.2  FAMILY BUSINESSES

The dynamic of a family business is more complex than standard businesses, but it can be even more rewarding. The experience is intensified with the emotional leverage of family and the work/life boundaries are often blurred.

You are specially initiated when (as a non-relative) you are employed by a family business. You're introduced to extended family members, friends, and a tight-knit community. Lunch and break times are communal as you break bread together. You can talk openly and freely about your own family. Birthdays and other milestones are always recognised. This personal approach means employees feel more invested because they feel part of the family. It's no longer "just a job" because you know that your fellow colleagues genuinely care.

This was certainly Chloe's experience during her time in a family business. She experienced a contrast between the typical agency life and working for a small family business. These early years fuelled her passion to have her own family business... Buttercrumble.

"Working here feels like being part of a family" may fill some people with dread. You picture a toxic work environment with no boundaries and a whole lot of blood, sweat, and tears. However, it doesn't need to be that way and the problems are not exclusive to family-owned businesses. It is the responsibility of the leaders to cultivate an empowering workplace and families have a unique position in creating inclusive, responsible environments.

McKinsey & Company (2010) highlighted several challenges with family-owned businesses including conflicts over money, nepotism, and succession struggles. Therefore, business owners must create fair strategies and policies with a meritocratic approach.

Family stakeholders tend to invest money back into the business rather than take large dividends. They have a heartfelt commitment to growth and are less likely to dilute ownership through distributing stock. Employees can do their work with the knowledge that personal development and business progression are taken seriously.

Multi-generational family businesses bring a wealth of insider experience as they may have been in the industry for decades. This said successful family businesses will consider fresh perspectives from other unrelated employees and external advisors to stay relevant.

A family business' long-term view makes it a more stable company to work for. They are less likely to take large financial risks that have brought many corporations to their knees. A stable cash flow is more important (to families) than higher risk and return. This approach has proved essential in weaker economic times and recessions.

Now, as a family business ourselves, we are dedicated to servicing our employees and design partners alike. There is a strong emotional connection among business colleagues and this has been a powerful motivator of profits and productivity. "Love" is not often associated with business, but it really makes a difference.

## 6.3   THE HIRING PROCESS

The hiring process feels like a swamp you have to wade through and you don't know what's lurking in the depths. "Look at that adorable frog– Oh, wait. It's an alligator!" One minute you'll be memorising hiring rules and regulations, and in the next minute you'll be analysing body language.

You can imagine that we were so excited, relieved, and grateful when we hired our first Creative Assistant. We believe the success of our first hire was bolstered by our branding as it helped us attract hundreds of positive candidates. A strong brand identity can recruit the perfect team, so taking some time to nurture it makes sense.

On the other hand, you cannot force your brand values upon people if they don't align with their own beliefs. Prioritise values over ability because — if you're vibing with someone — it's much easier to teach them the technical skills! When we invited our Creative Assistant to join Buttercrumble, we knew she'd fit right in from her passion for creativity and young-at-heart vibe. It's instinctive, so listen carefully to your gut which can decode the energies of others.

We must admit that we've found the process of building a team difficult. Yes, we preach the importance of vision, but it's not always so simple. Your vision could be as clear-as-crystal and some people won't follow it.

You need your team to follow your vision and not their own. We see Buttercrumble as an enabler for our community to live out their own dreams, but whilst on task, we need to be unified in Buttercrumble's vision. People who can follow your vision translate to great leaders who will push the business in the right direction (and not the direction they want).

## CHLOE'S REFLECTION

❝ How do you get your team to buy into your vision? They say passion is infectious and you should lead by example. I don't think it's that easy to find people who believe in the business as passionately as you do though. If Buttercrumble is a living and breathing extension of us, why hasn't the love we poured in filtered into our team? We don't care for dilution.

Furthermore, we have always been complimented on our company culture but this is something we need to learn to define. Our culture was so intrinsic to us, the founders, I don't know if it translates to work culture. We are young and have had little experience in an office or agency environment.

When hiring we were so keen to bring in someone who shared our culture and attitude that we ended up with duplicate skills. We felt that technical ability could be trained whilst personality could not. However, this approach didn't plug our skills gap. We noticed a drift in personality, maybe we were naive to take the enthusiasm of an interview for granted. Over time, this bubbly creativity was diluted and I wonder if, in a small business, you need someone with grit. It's a hard slog and everyone has to pull their socks up.

Just like in theatre, there's no such thing as a small part. Every team member is essential to the brand story. We spent a lot of time sharing our journey with the team to help them understand and empathise with the business mission. We need ambassadors who can tell the brand story like it's second nature.

. . . . . . . . . . . . . . . . . .

An increasing number of organisations recognise the importance of diversity and inclusion within their teams.

A diverse team can help to provide additional insights into the worlds of your customers and clients. We all have unique perspectives and ethnicities and backgrounds different from your own may be able to provide more empathetic connections, and in turn, make your organisation more effective and profitable.

Global management consultancy, McKinsey & Company (2020), continue to emphasise the importance of diversity and inclusion within teams. They believe an inclusive work environment bolsters employee engagement, resulting in increased retention, productivity, and financial performance.

We appreciate the importance of a diverse workplace and know this has been a weakness. As twin founders, we've experienced life through the same lens, our perspective is very narrow. This is why we're passionate about nurturing a diverse team. However, achieving this has been more difficult than anticipated. Our applicant pool for opportunities looks just like ours!

Buttercrumble is looking at ways we can create a more inclusive environment. We believe we can achieve this by promoting fairness and transparency in recruitment. We're also nurturing our open culture which is essential to creativity. There is no risk in sharing ideas — we want to welcome discussion and feedback. At Buttercrumble, we want to encourage and uplift our community to be themselves!

**If you want to increase diversity in your team, you could:**
- ★ Recruit from different places and platforms
- ★ Reach out to schools
- ★ Support minority businesses and initiatives
- ★ Promote diverse imagery

It's important to note that a diverse hire is not your golden ticket to success as building the right team takes patience and dedication. You can get so hung up on introducing new skill sets and perspectives into the team that you can forget your company's vision. Despite our best intentions, we hired the wrong fit, and it forced us to reflect on our culture. We value creativity, communication, and collaboration and if a candidate does not share all three values, we cannot introduce them to our team. It made us realise that culture and attitude come first, and competency comes second. This competency can be developed if the candidate has the right attitude.

The business can feel like an albatross, it's all down to you, and you can't quit. There are things you don't understand but you can be criticised and held accountable for them. You can have the best intentions of the business at heart but you can't predict the effects. It's been a trial-and-error experience for us. But, we have learnt more in this small amount of time starting the business, than we ever could have in "normal" jobs.

Overall, the team is impacting your customer's brand perceptions, so it's best to make sure everyone is on board with your organisation's missions and values.

There can be a great sense of camaraderie in teams and this is something we always shared as co-founders and wanted to extend to new members. This was felt when we arrived at the studio one morning to see "Happy Birthday" bunting on display and gifts on our desks. How lovely it feels to be recognised by your employees as a boss or a manager. Unlike times before, we knew we were cultivating the right team for Buttercrumble.

## 6.4  YOUR SUPPLIERS

We all know the phrase, "jack of all trades and master of none", simply, we can't do it all (perfectly)! Often in business, we have to call on suppliers to help us do our job. At Buttercrumble, we don't outsource a lot, but we are so lucky to have built a strong network of experts. Believe it or not, branding can play a huge part in this!

Collaboration makes us better. By forming genuine relationships with our suppliers, we can build trust. We only outsource to those we can count on. Moreover, when said suppliers adopt a similar brand identity to ourselves, we know our clients will feel safer. After all, familiarity breeds a sense of comfort. When clients are parting with their hard-earned money, it makes sense to offer peace of mind. It's a no-brainer!

Overall, you can think of your network of suppliers as a deck of cards. All cards sit harmoniously together within the deck because of their aligning values. However, each has something new to bring to the table. You can call on them when you need to.

One of our most pleasurable projects of 2019 was when we were granted the opportunity to collaborate with — Jessica Grady — our friend and fellow beach babe (Jess is from Whitby). We met Jess at a mentorship programme in 2017. Together we participated in a year-long scholarship to improve our creative business skills and hit it off. We were approached to create the interpretation for a museum exhibition, commenting on sustainability. We knew the perfect partner to help us create the wow factor. It was a pleasure to commission Jessica and our collaboration helped to raise awareness around our ocean's health. We wanted to cultivate a business which allowed us to work with people we love and value; it was a pleasure to bring Jessica on board with such a meaningful project.

Jessica is an embroidery artist who utilises mixed media and recycled materials so beautifully. She uses painted metal washers, hand-dyed plastic cotton buds, dyed sponges and stripped electric cables, to name a few delights. These materials are transformed and manipulated to create intricate embellishments. The unusual techniques and vibrant colours drew us to Jess' work in addition to our shared love of the East Coast.

## ABIGAIL'S REFLECTION

66 One gem in Buttercrumble's crown came from a chance encounter on social media. Bing! We had received a direct message on Instagram from a Midlands maverick called Gaz.

Ting! A direct message had landed in Buttercrumble's Instagram inbox and we had to check it out. It was a request to showcase our business — free of charge — because our story had resonated with a local social media guru and photographer. Although it was strategic for them, it was a bonus for us too. In this world, we gotta help each other, right?

We obliged. By getting to know Gaz, the photographer, we were able to receive our brand film — free of charge! This may sound too good to be true, but it came from growing a friendship. There were no coercion tactics or special promises. Simply, our values resonated with one another. We were able to support Gaz too.

When we'd had no prior relationship, I wholeheartedly believe that branding had a part to play in the success of this union. People are naturally drawn to those of similar beliefs. Its psychological term is "consensual validation". We enjoy meeting people who share our values as it increases our confidence. To attract like-minded suppliers, you need to be conveying values you admire. You will find others can echo this.

Businesses display their values through their brand identity and messaging. It was clear to Gaz that we were approachable. After all, we are regularly communicating our willingness to collaborate. To prove this, we even created a fresh brand identity for Gaz as a way to return the favour.

I always say people are sent as a blessing or a lesson, and it's up to you to figure that out along the way. For your suppliers, you're looking for blessings! These are the supporters who are going to boost your business and help you perform at your best. We're fortunate for all the lovely organisations we've had the pleasure of partnering with.

. . . . . . . . . . . . . . . . . .

## 6.5   YOUR CUSTOMERS

The world is changing and businesses can't rely on traditional selling methods. It's no longer enough to persuade your audience through flashy advertisements. You must make yourself useful and indispensable by providing a platform to your customers. A platform doesn't need to deduce their customers, they earn support by making life easier.

You can obsess over your competition, you can use traditional positioning techniques, and you can employ intensive marketplace research. This will gain you success. However, obsessing over your audience will take you further. Focus on your purpose and how you can fulfil both your employee and customer needs.

**Exceptional customer experience = brand loyalty.** This is the holy grail that brand builders are striving for and customer experience is intrinsic to branding. How do customers perceive their interactions with your brand — online and offline? At Buttercrumble, we often chime "We create designs to make us smile, our clients smile and in turn, their customers smile too". You better expect smiling faces at Buttercrumble as we have to deliver on our promise.

Customers are already confused about what they may need or want. Don't confuse them with unclear messaging and a confused brand. They truly want security and a return on their investment. Consider how your customers may expect you to behave based on your organisation's branding. The tone of voice plays a vital role in this, For example, is your organisation caring, knowledgeable and attentive? Or is your organisation enthusiastic, confident and amicable? If you match (or exceed) customer expectations, you can build a good rapport.

Disney is renowned for their magical "guestology". The brand has increased in strength with thanks to its approach to customer experience. Disney uses "The Compass" method to train their employees to appreciate and understand customers as individuals (Harvard

Business Review, 2018). All Cast Members (staff) are guided by the same process, so feel united. It inspires them to go the extra mile.

The Compass points to Needs (North), Emotions (East), Wants (West) and Stereotypes (South). Crew Members are trained to keep all of these elements in mind when treating a customer (Fast Company, 2013). This methodology encourages the staff to ask questions and to actively listen to responses.

This type of strategy content would form the organisation's "Behavioural Guidelines". These may be included in your overall brand guidelines or training documents. It helps to nurture a service which may be consistently and correctly delivered. If the perfect method is communicated clearly, everyone who processes this can then strive toward perfection in every customer interaction.

If you'd like to follow in Disney's footsteps and begin building customer experience into your overall strategy, evaluate where you are currently. For example, in your specific industry, do any other organisations set the gold standard? Who are the true customer carers? What may prevent you from providing a brilliant experience?

Customer journey mapping should be another essential part of your research. To achieve this, focus on the different touch-points a customer may encounter when experiencing your brand. At each point, think about what the different interactions may be. This will clarify what questions a customer may raise and any actions you can take to support the buying process.

The first stage of a customer journey requires special attention. Do you know what your customers are looking for? Go back to your value proposition and confirm that you are delivering solutions to real and current problems. Then research where customers are discovering you. This is as simple as asking prospects "Where did you find out about us?" If you're running an online business, you could include this question in your contact form or when users sign up for your email newsletter subscription.

The journey often follows Attention, Interest, Desire and Action (AIDA). For example, you grab their attention when your social media post shows within their news feed. They click through to your website, interested in your content. They desire your services, so they enquire through your contact form. Finally, there is the action (or transaction) when they invest in your brand! You may also think about extending the journey through a loyalty or referral scheme. Retaining customers will save your company money in the long term! One in the hand is worth two in the bush. Evaluate each of these stages to map out a fruitful customer journey.

## 6.6   ALL ONBOARD!

However, it's no use to make these changes if your team isn't on board with the process. This is why it's important to monitor standards across the organisation. Have a quality management system in place which communicates the monitoring standards and expectations. This is how you can shift from an organisation where service is exceptional sometimes, to every time. With quality control in place, you can focus on a procedure where the delivery of customer service is both consistent and exceptional.

And — hey — we see you solopreneurs taking a French exit! Even if you have no plans to grow your team, it's important that you keep yourself accountable. This exercise might be more helpful than you think.

The behavioural guidelines, brand messaging and quality management system need to be communicated to the team regularly. Everyone from the cleaners to the directors needs to be fully invested in the customer experience. This is not just a job for your sales assistants. For new team members, create a brand-driven approach to training and inductions. You need to be reviewing with the team regularly to ensure everyone is still on board with your organisation's strategy.

We all have boundaries (literally and metaphorically) in place within an organisation. These are there for reasons. However, sometimes customers may want to step past this point. They must be able to explain clearly to the customer why this rule or policy is in place to resolve any conflict. If not, you'll have to face potentially dire consequences.

If employees do not understand the process and quality management system, they may improvise and compromise the brand's tone of voice and essence when a challenge is raised by a customer. When a customer realises the team member is unsure, they will request to speak to a manager. The situation escalates.

Customer experience is public and it only takes one angry customer to tarnish your reputation with a poor review. It's natural for a customer's emotions to become heightened when they feel their expectations have not met reality. However, these things do happen and you can't be everyone's cup of tea. Show you can see the person, as well as the potential issues. The person wants to feel listened to and understood. Other people will see your response to the challenge and make a judgement based on this. The audience will respect a graceful response.

When customers feel seen, understood and valued, they will happily invest in the organisation. You will see results as brand ambassadors begin to spread the word about how they were treated.

To keep driving your customer experience strategy forward, have a plan for dealing with errors caused by yourself or the team. Remember to celebrate your successes too.

Your customer service can not be easily replicated. It's a part of your brand DNA. It is the personality of your people and company, combined. Connecting with customers on an emotional level is essential to separate yourself from competitors. This links directly with your brand identity and strategy. It's about resonating with your audience on a personal level. When you understand the person and their many unique layers, you can offer a high level of sensitivity and genuine care.

**Wait! How Do You Build a Customer Base?**

OK, OK, so we know it's tricky when you're first starting from a customer base of zero. From our experience, the best way to build is: be kind. People do business with people. We are all sharing this planet and on a life journey together. You can't do everything on your own and sooner or later you will need help. We have been fortunate to receive the support of many talented, experienced, and wise people over the years. From teachers to family members, from friends to colleagues, everybody has their own golden nugget to share. We are not saying all advice you receive is gospel — take some words with a pinch of salt! By being open-minded and a critical-thinker you can make the best decision for you and your business.

## CHLOE'S REFLECTION

❝ Buttercrumble has received support from people who were part of our journey before the business. In our first year, we were invited to illustrate shoppers at Leeds' Corn Exchange, our drawing tutor from our first year of University approached us and exclaimed, "I remember you in my class and now look at you"! The guidance we received whilst studying has informed us today.

We have also received support from our colleagues at work and have received amazing recommendations from those we worked with. By being honest, we could build meaningful relationships with the people we worked with (including our bosses). I have met small business owners who chose to keep their new venture private, sometimes out of legal necessity, sometimes out of fear of judgement, this is understandable. We felt blessed by all the creative organisations we worked for, the teams were totally supportive of Buttercrumble and uplifted us. A candle loses nothing by lighting another candle and we have been fortunate to meet people who share this ethos.

When I handed my notice in, I felt sick with nerves! I absolutely loved both the briefs I completed and the colleagues who surrounded me. I had to make a choice though. We had cultivated and nurtured so many design projects that they could no longer be contained to the evenings, more clients were asking to meet-in-person, and my annual leave had already been dedicated to this. I could take the leap now, or down-size the business. We wanted to take a chance.

My boss sighed with relief when I explained my reasons for leaving. "I am so honoured you told me, thank you", she smiled. I wasn't leaving to join a competitor, I wasn't leaving because I hated the work. I was leaving because — in a way — I was following in my boss' footsteps. They respected my entrepreneurial spirit.

With speed, my first creative employment heard the word on the grapevine. The connections I made in PR completely embody the meaning of the word and they practised what they preach. A friend recommended me to their relative who happened to be a successful journalist and television personality. This was a fantastic break to receive and we continued to collaborate with that client over a number of years. To have such a renowned client on our books added great kudos. We always say, "it's not what you know, it's not who you know, it's who knows you"! By taking small, simple steps to nurture relationships and create a good first impression, you can collaborate and support one another.

Impress your peers and impress your managers. Two years into our journey, a former manager approached us for design support! I felt honoured to be considered when they have no shortage in their network. We continue to collaborate with this client as their skills are transferable and valued by our own clients. Together, we have created a beautiful working relationship and we are always on the look-out for relevant opportunities for our clients.

Now, I realise I am painting a rose-tinted image of the world we live in, take care. Many people we've met on our journey have been a blessing, some people have provided a lesson as we mentioned earlier.

In our first year, we were approached by a media personality who invited us to their home. Their communication seemed light and friendly, we were excited by their expertise and the things we seemingly had in common. "The start of a beautiful friendship" we cried! However, the rushed hospitality and over-friendliness reflected the stressful nature of the work ahead. There were no professional boundaries. Beware of clients that need to know every minute detail of your business, and your future plans, and insist on favours. When a client believes buying you a coffee warrants free design-work, say "no way José"! Of course, some people are showing genuine interest, but some may be a wolf in sheep's clothing.

· · · · · · · · · · · · · · · · · ·

We are often asked if it's important to include self-initiated, passion projects in portfolios, as a strategy to attract the right audience. In a way, developing Buttercrumble's brand is a self-initiated project. We're constantly trying to develop the business in creative ways through our branding and marketing. We also practise illustration outside of client projects. After all, it was our love of illustration which fuelled our motivation to establish a design studio.

In recent times, there is pressure for everything you enjoy to become a "side hustle". However, it's liberating to have an actual hobby with no commercial pressure. If you love making things, keep doing it! Have those passion projects for yourself and you'll find your skills just keep on improving.

Do tailor your offering to your clients — but — don't create offerings on assumptions. It's important to listen to your marketplace as your tastes may not be the most commercial.

## 6.7 CUSTOMER FEEDBACK

Customer or client feedback can be highly beneficial in identifying blind spots and, on the other hand, growth opportunities. You have the power to generate more business opportunities and boost satisfaction when a negative comment is carefully negated.

We request constructive feedback from prospects — whenever our proposals are rejected — and this inspires innovation. For example, a business coach shared the "analysis paralysis" he experienced when reviewing our services. We presented him with too many options and he felt overwhelmed by the amount of information within our proposal. We considered this dilemma for a while and decided to simplify the layout and structure of our proposals. As a business owner (and expert in your field) it's easy to forget the customer's green perspective.

After this, we implemented "Crumble Bundles" to summarise the recommended services in a more palatable way. This has increased our conversion rate as it's much easier for a customer to request "Bundle one" than list all the different services they require.

Feedback can be a bitter pill, but it has the power to make you better. Everybody needs to learn how and when to take feedback onboard. After all, not all feedback will be relevant and it's your job to distinguish what's right and what's wrong for YOU. The choice words of one individual may not be representative of your wider community as a whole. Use one negative comment, not as law, but as a prompt to gather more feedback and illustrate a better picture of your marketplace.

You may hear an amazing suggestion for a special offer or service that you're eager to implement. However — stop for one second — and consider its feasibility. Does the suggestion fit within your business model or is it just a distraction? There will be times when you have to work within the practical limitations of your business… Put that idea on the back-burner.

Feedback can feel extremely personal (as a business owner) because of the effort we commit to our product or service. However, one must disconnect and view the critique objectively. If you want to truly serve your customers, you need to let go of your ego and give the people what they want! We don't believe in the cliché "the customer is always right" but there is an ounce of wisdom in it.

## CHLOE'S REFLECTION

❝ I worked for a discerning employer in my paper-craft days. These were happy times when I'd collaborate with my senior designer to create beautiful patterns, motifs, and embellishments for card-making. It was rewarding to see our designs sell on a popular daytime shopping channel.

Television shopping is a fast-paced and demanding world. Our channel worked on a sale or return basis which means they would place a huge order and then if it didn't sell, we'd be burdened with the inventory and manufacturing costs. It was imperative that the products sold in order to maintain the TV deal, generate turnover, and reduce inventory.

I really admired my senior designer and she taught me a lot about commerciality, as did my employer. We'd generate concepts in double-time and I'd have to climb the stairs to my boss' office in order to present our ideas. Each time, she would shake her head and send me away with amendments to complete. I always accepted the feedback gracefully (despite being very proud of the visuals) because I knew my employer was right. I respected her decades of experience.

Furthermore, she really knew her customers. She regularly invited ladies into the factory shop for weekend craft sessions and she dedicated a lot of time to chatting with her customers at different trade shows. Gosh — one loyal customer even had lunch with the staff every week and we're now Facebook friends! (That's how you know it's official)!

We even had craft ambassadors who received free products to test and enjoy. The projects they crafted acted as a form of user-generated-content for the brand to market. We also listened to their feedback intently.

I've been employed by some big worldwide brands, but none of them matched that employer's dedication to her customers. Her feedback never came from a place of petty criticism, but from commercial knowledge, and an understanding of our customer needs.

I'd monitor the customer feedback, following every collection launch, on social media. Guess what? My boss was right! We had real brand fans who felt seen, heard, and valued.

Boy, these early days gave me a thick skin! I look forward to hearing real feedback as, like a phoenix rising from the ashes, it helps you flourish. I've met with clients who use expletives to describe my deliverables and they are well within their rights to do so. Bring it on! It's never personal, just a matter of taste. We nurture our relationships, actively encourage transparency and, in turn, it allows us to get the best results for our clients. The support is mutual and — in return — we receive new, lucrative opportunities.

. . . . . . . . . . . . . . . . . .

Feedback can be easily generated through surveys, however statistics and structured data won't paint a full picture. Let's face it — your customer is not a structured statistic. Human beings are messy and complex beings who need their unique story to be understood. Thus, interviews can be key to unlocking an in-depth understanding of your customers' experience as they allow you to pose follow-up questions for extra insight.

Try social listening if you prefer to work incognito. This stealth-mode approach involves you monitoring and analysing social media for reviews and comments. Social listening is fruitful for large B2C companies where customers are more open about their purchases.

There are few opportunities for B2B reviews as customers are secretive. Businesses don't always want their end consumers to know that they're outsourcing services.

If you've cultivated a community for your brand, think about setting up a WhatsApp group to receive customer feedback. Here, you can encourage people to share comments related to specific areas of concern and it builds trust through exclusive and responsive support. Your customers become your co-creators and, in turn, your cheerleaders.

Trends can change quickly and the business landscape continues to evolve. Feedback is a strategic tool you must utilise alongside your own intuition. You need to create a balanced decision to guarantee long-term success, and not just a quick win for one customer.

^     *In 2019, we created this mural at the international industry show, Playtime*
*Paris. We illustrated those we met and added them to the family tree artwork that*
*grew over three days. Here, we met many new friends, including the founder of*
*Light+Nine, whom we still love to collaborate with today.*

*People always giggle when we tell them our USA exporting journey began in Paris.*
*You never know where or when you'll meet new partners.*

# Chapter 7

# IMPLEMENTATION

*Make it matter.*

---

You've got your value proposition, you've adopted your tone of voice, and you've refined your strategy. After months of deliberation, it's time to get your brand out there in the world, and lead the way. This is the marketing aspect of business, where you can build a community interested in you, your product and or service.

Yet, even at this point, there can be hesitation. Self-promotion is tough! You don't want to be seen as a "big-head". After all, our parents always told us not to boast. Yet, we must remember that confidence is not about being high and mighty. It's a peaceful security, where you know you're capable and have something of worth to offer to the world. Now is not the time to hide away.

It's time to have a mindset shift around self-promotion, and turn "I can't" into "I can". Your work is valuable and you can positively impact people's lives, so let's expand that value. However, solely doing the work is not enough to grow a sustainable business — especially if you're starting from scratch. People are so consumed with their own lives, they may not notice. So, you have to bring attention to your benefits to build a name for yourself. You'll need to market yourself to gain that first special customer.

Some people are embarrassed of appearing as a "try-hard". If you do, at least you're trying to do something useful with your time. Critics may think you're trying too hard even if you do nothing. Face it, everyone has an opinion about everything, so don't sweat it. Remind yourself of your mission and vision, and go for it.

You absolutely can get ahead once you start to put your plan into action, and implement it!

## 7.1   TANGIBLE ASSETS (IDENTITY AND TOUCH-POINTS)

We live in a society where looks are important. Why else can consumers identify a magazine advertisement for Cadbury Chocolate — instantly — without seeing the brand name? How do we spot a Louis Vuitton bag at ten paces? Or recognise Tiffany & Co through colour alone? We can process a plethora of visual messages within a heartbeat, with no need for explicit explanation, non-verbal cues play an essential role in our lives.

A brand's visual touch-points act as signposts which alert us, as consumers, whether an organisation is for us (or not). In this content-heavy, fast-paced world, we are making snap judgements based on first impressions. Thoughtful design can inspire curiosity and unshakeable loyalty. If we can make an emotional connection, we may feel the company is worth our time.

Additionally, visual reminders are a great way to express your brand values to the team. In this digital age, ensure you are presenting the identity across your online collaboration tools. Your branding can be carried across your emails and project management systems. However, technology has taken over and we're losing the human element within our organisations. Let's combat this and consider the physical realm — it is just as important. To develop a personal touch, you need tangible assets. Touch-points to consider are: workplace decor, staff room, branded mailers, brochures, thank you notes, well-presented packaging, exhibitions and interactive demonstrations. Use these as a vehicle for your mission. If you display your vision publicly within and around the business' premises, it becomes a motivating manifesto for all invested in the organisation.

# TOUCHPOINT WHEEL

*Activity*

—

Check each asset off as it is added to your guidelines:

☑

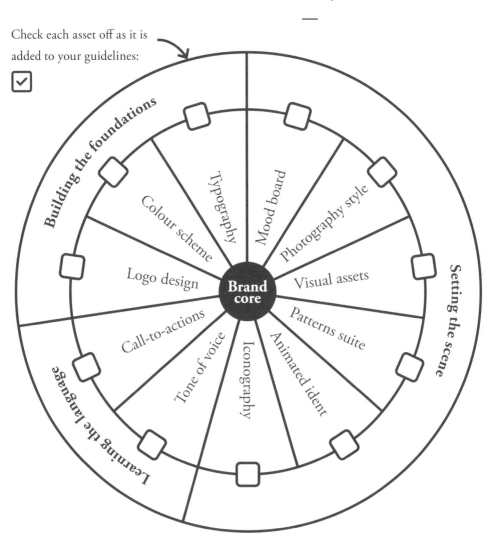

The brand core (strategy) is at the hub, and should inform all your touchpoints.

Each spoke acts as a page for your guidelines. Can you collect them all?

## 7.2  THE FACE OF YOUR BRAND

We can all acknowledge the importance of aesthetics. In this noisy-visual-world, how can you ensure your message is heard? Thoughtful, strategic branding is crucial to marketing success. Naturally, you won't be an overnight sensation, you won't be instantly recognisable, and you'll be unable to trademark the colour pink. It takes time to build your visual brand identity and you must commit, respect, and love it.

At Buttercrumble, we're creative people, looking for the hottest new thing. However, if we swapped and changed our brand every time our feet itched, we wouldn't be as recognisable as we are now. Our audience recognises us thanks to a magical blend of our tangible brand assets which we've respected since Autumn 2015.

However, this level of commitment doesn't mean you have to let your branding go stale. You must weigh up the pros and cons of rebranding and find sophisticated ways to refresh and excite your customers. There are many ingredients to consider within your brand identity and you must nurture and evaluate each one. The tangible assets are:

- ★ Logo design: The emblem your brand wears proudly
- ★ Colour scheme: Sustain your brand with consistent colour
- ★ Typography: The fonts your brand uses to communicate
- ★ Visual assets: Extra brand visuals such as small illustrations
- ★ Mood board: Outline your aesthetic with a mood board
- ★ Patterns: A suite of patterns are great for adding visual interest
- ★ Ident: See your branding in motion with an animated logo
- ★ Tone of voice: Ensure your audience responds positively to your copy
- ★ Iconography: Highlight key information and values with brand icons
- ★ Call-to-action: What do you want your audience to do when they see your brand?
- ★ Photography style: Show attention to detail with coherent photography

## 7.3   MAKING MEANING

For many, these tangible assets are the exciting part of branding, but don't let yourself get caught up in the fun. Separate yourself and personal tastes from the business as you may not be your own customer. Take care to imagine your audience; what would they like to see? Don't underestimate the value of customer insights. Design is a super-power you can use to communicate with your customers on a deeper, subconscious, and emotional level.

When a brand is so strong, you no longer have to read its name and logo. Instead, you see, feel and know it. It's instantly recognisable. When you put your heart into your brand, people can't help but stop and notice because it holds emotion.

To clarify, your imagery should support feelings and resonance. According to revered art director, David Crow (2003) images are vehicles of message and meaning which your audience subconsciously decodes. This is called semiology (a general science of signs). It is a theory proposed in the early 1900s by a Swiss professor and American philosopher named Saussure and Peirce, respectively. They were concerned with the theory of how a sign sends a message which we can understand and how the meaning of that sign is formed. British visual semiotician, David Chandler (2014) explains how Saussure's model involved the 'signifier' which is a word or image and the 'signified' is the connotations of that word or image. When discussing the signified, it may be denotative or connotative. Denotations are the factual meanings of a sign, whereas connotations are more personal associations of the sign. For example, the heart is an organ which pumps blood throughout the body, however it connotes love and warmth which is why it is a popular visual for brand communications. Everyone has differing associations with signs which is why your identity can affect the way your audience feels.

**What's the difference between the signifier and signified?**

Signifier: the word (or image).

Signified: the meaning (factual or personal associations).

People often carry emotions with their personal associations, so you may be able to leverage this depending on what you want to convey and communicate through your logo.

Whilst on the topic of logos, it's a good time to consider the difference between logos, symbols and signs. Logo is a shortened version of the Greek word "logotype" which may be translated as "word imprint". A symbol can not be a logo by itself as it is a conventional representation of an object, function, or process. However, with persistence and consistency, a brand can make a symbol its own — just think of Shell and Nike. You need to utilise a strong symbol and gain a large spread of awareness before the symbol can become a distinctive asset for a company. Finally, a sign has limited room for interpretation (such as a number or written word). All elements can convey meaning, so use them wisely.

If you want to make an emotional impact, use colour. In extreme examples, the colour becomes a brand asset to be fiercely protected because it plays a huge part in physical branding. For example, Tiffany & Co own a trademark on their instantly recognisable turquoise blue. Other brands have also taken legal action to protect their colour such as Starbucks and Christopher Louboutin (who fought to prevent imitators from adopting his famous red soles).

Be careful with the signs, symbols and colours you use. Context can make-or-break your brand! The meaning of an image changes depending on what one sees around it and their existing cultural associations. This is why, when designing your brand identity, you must be careful. You need to ensure your intended message is understood. Your visuals may appear pointless, outdated or irrelevant for those outside of the appropriate audience (such as a different culture or ethnicity). For example, white symbolises innocence and peace in western countries. However, in some eastern regions, it is bad luck and used when mourning. Always keep culture in mind, be inclusive and avoid any visual faux-pas!

Come what may, consider the cultural, emotional, and psychological meanings your branding could have with your audience.

## 7.4   DIGITAL APPLICATIONS

It's the modern world and the way consumers engage with brands has changed. Many traditional strategies for designers and marketers are becoming obsolete… we can no longer rely on the old way of doing business!

For instance, let's examine a shoe shopper's experience pre-internet. The consumer would hit the high-street, interacting with brands through their shop-windows, visual merchandising, and store assistants. There would be a limited amount of choices to consider and the consumer would pick the most suitable option for their needs. A great customer assistant would guide the customer and finalise the sale. David C. Edelman, respected marketing advisor, describes how the buyer's relationship with the store assistant and brand would "typically dissipate after the purchase" (2010, p.2) but times have changed. Edelman elaborates that consumers are now continuously connecting with brands through new and varying media channels. They have endless choices to aggressively pursue and narrow. Consumers are more public in their promotion or criticism of brands. Consumers engage less with shop windows, visual merchandising, and store assistants, so business owners need to realign their strategy with new touchpoints.

**New digital touchpoint to consider for your brand include:**

- ★ Messaging apps
- ★ Social media platforms
- ★ Chat-bots
- ★ Experiential websites
- ★ Online marketplaces
- ★ Blogs
- ★ Digital advertising
- ★ Email newsletters

Although consumers are interacting with brands through increasing touch-points, they still expect the same quality of interaction... If not, better! New platforms enable a closer level of connectivity between brands and consumers. We are holding brands to a higher standard than ever before as they have access to the most personal details of our lives. With touch-points like social media comes a new-found responsibility so brands need to display transparency, integrity, and genuine interest in their customers' needs.

## 7.5   SIGN OF THE TIMES

If you want to remain relevant, the ability to read the room is an essential skill to have. Irrelevance will see you exit stage left quicker than you can say "trend forecasting".

Trend forecasting is about taking a temperature check of culture in the now and future. This is an essential survival skill for any business to help you anticipate consumer tastes and innovate for the better. Creatives often have a precondition for this, with their need to question the world around them.

Think of our stars and planets. They began as clouds of dust, scattered throughout the galaxies. Particles began to cluster, ultimately building upon themselves until they attracted larger masses. This is cultural adoption.

Many businesses can be risk-averse (us included). So, trend forecasting can soothe these anxieties and solve problems. Predictions can give us a sense of certainty, which in turn, assists our strategy. By partnering with a creative consultant, you can filter the bombardment of messages on the internet, and get to what's right for you. Once you know where the world is heading, you can plan backwards to stay pertinent.

When designing new brands, we aim to get clients on board with modernity. However, time and time again, we hear "we don't want to be trendy" or "I'm not interested in what's fashionable". Yet, they fail to recognise that there are different types of trends: micro and macro.

**What is a micro trend?**

This is what clients are referring to with their disdain for what's vogue. Micro trends refer to short-term shifts in consumer behaviour that sometimes feel narrow, such as fidget spinners and yo-yos. Fads aren't always bad though! They are often linked to an overarching macro trend of the time, so can give us quick indications of how consumer taste is transforming.

**What is a macro trend?**

A macro trend is a long-term change in the business landscape, created by shifts in society's behaviour. They impact numerous sectors simultaneously and adjust over time. These are important to pay attention to because they demonstrate human needs such as population ageing and climate action. All the more, people are concerned with the future — it's something we need to address.

Now, there is a difference between dated and classic brands. When we think of something dated, we describe it as archaic and old-fashioned — these are negative connotations, right? Whereas, the classics are seen as established, ageless and exemplary. They still feel relevant because they have grasped onto a basic human need or value, whilst subtly pivoting over time.

For example, Tiffany & Co was born in 1837, yet they are still jewellery magnates. They have achieved this through their consistent, beautiful blue presentation and timeless attention to detail. Yet, they do progress with the times. In 2018, they launched a new Manhattan-based lab to ramp up innovation and create punchier collections for a younger audience. The new space has improved productivity as the designers are making the product mock-ups in conjunction with marketing and sales teams at the headquarters (within walking distance) (Bloomberg, 2018). This design innovation can transform stodgy sales into a profit plant.

So, macro trends are set to influence the key creative decisions you must make. The timing of this is vital. Although we're focussing on design and brand positioning, future foresight will influence your business across all areas including research and development, marketing and sales.

We understand that no one wants to be the flavour of just one month. Hence, how do you spot changing tastes? Trend forecasters have a talent for the semiotic reading of imagery. Visual language is an important stimulation for ideas. Therefore, consider what research tools you can use when designing your brand. You might:

★ Visit stores to see what's new
★ Talk to the experts or raving fans
★ Conduct traditional desk research
★ Source trend reports
★ Sign up for relevant newsletters

It is constant research (and you may already do it unknowingly). It inspires and aids business decisions, just as branding does. It prepares you for navigating changing systematic values.

Intuition is also your friend, as you must nurture the ability to sense when the tide is changing. As you know — inspiration can strike at the most random of times. You have to imagine the possibilities that are yet to happen, with support from cold hard facts. If your brand is a disruptor, ground-breaker or maverick, communicate that you're ahead of the curve through design.

Essentially, you want to show you're a champion of the consumer, who's set to inspire their world as you have your finger on the pulse. Your visual aesthetic should reflect the cultural climate at the time of creation.

As a brand, this offers a major opportunity to do good! The world is realigning due to technological, social, and environmental issues. There are broken systems that design can begin to heal. Design your brand to aid the improvement of society. Be a future maker.

## 7.6   CURATE YOUR ASSETS

You have spent months consulting and deliberating on your brand design. Blood, sweat, and tears have gone into the creation of your identity. It's finally primed — ready to be embraced by your customers — and you cannot wait. The branding process takes time and financial commitment. Naturally, you're desperate to put this branding to good use, nobody wants to waste their resources. Yet, so many businesses rush into a thriftless trap where they fail to follow brand guidelines. It becomes a free-for-all for all those communicating on behalf of the company.

Really, your tangible assets should be compiled into easy-to-follow brand guidelines. Use this bible and you will see your brand's full potential. By following guidelines, your team can help maintain a coherent brand. The guide can be referred to when creating any new brand visuals. It saves you time and money in the long-term as design decisions become automatic and second-nature.

**Top tip:** Print your guidelines out and have them professionally bound. You can now display it in your work space so it's always in mind.

Don't leave your guidelines in your desk drawers, you need to stay in touch with your brand. Make it a pleasure and joy by creating a positive narrative about the brand's life which inspires you and your team to feel enthusiastic about their roles.

## 7.7   PROTECT YOUR ASSETS

What other measures can you put in place to maintain and protect the integrity of your brand? Let's face it, building your business is hard work, and you want to protect your success. We are often asked about intellectual property and how businesses can protect their product and brand. Are they automatically entitled to protection? Do we retain the rights? Can they change their design? There is so much to consider but it doesn't need to be complicated.

Over the years, Buttercrumble has received wonderful support from the British Library's Business and IP Centre (in addition to our legal eagle friends). We would always advise our clients to seek professional advice for their business' intellectual property but let's take a look at the foundations!

At the time of writing, intellectual property law (within the United Kingdom) states that 'design right' ensures automatic protection. This means any designs you create are protected for 10 years from the moment it was first sold or 15 years after its creation — whichever comes soonest! However, this automatic protection of unregistered designs only seeks to protect the form of expression of ideas, not the ideas themselves. Moreover, similar designs may exist as long as they haven't been copied.

To qualify, your design must be original and uncommon. This means the design must be your own work and not broadly recognised within a group of similar products. Be careful because there are some exemptions! For example, the Intellectual Property Office (IPO) also states that 2D designs such as textile patterns, graphics, and wallpaper do not qualify for automatic UK design rights.

You can prove you created your design by leaving copies of your design drawings with your bank or solicitor; or mail them to yourself by registered, dated post and left unopened. These measures ensure clear-cut, indefinite proof of your ownership.

We are often asked about design ownership as generally, the person who created the design owns the intellectual property, however when the design is commissioned the commissioner will often own the right unless otherwise stated.

At Buttercrumble, upon completion of the services and full payment of all fees and costs due, we grant the client the exclusive, perpetual and worldwide right and licence to use, reproduce and display the works solely in connection with the project as defined in the proposal. We clearly state the level of modification allowed to the design and every piece of work we produce is bespoke to the client. This is to guarantee peace of mind for everyone involved.

If you require further protection, you could register your design. We recommend registering assets as trademarks. They are used to differentiate goods or services and can comprise of: words, letters, colours and numbers (to name but a few)!

You can register processes and devices as a patent. This can be more expensive than seeking to protect as a trade secret but some innovations are too good to maintain as secrets. They can also be more challenging to register as the invention must be new, involve an inventive step, be capable of industrial application and is not specifically excluded from protection as a patent.

When inventing or dreaming up new designs — there is no need to fear! By taking simple steps, and the advice of legal professionals, you can guarantee the protection of your design. Many designers appreciate and respect the needs of their clients and will work with you to ensure your vision is realised.

## 7.8   BRANDING ON A BUDGET

As a start-up you need to think big, act small! The scale of your budget might not meet the scale of your vision… Don't despair! When every penny counts, you are more likely to consider your spends carefully and, in turn, invest wisely. In the early days, you are developing your entrepreneurial skills, testing your idea, and getting to know your customers. This time is essential so don't let go of your grand vision… It can drive you to success.

Visually-captivating graphics are a linchpin of a successful brand, however you don't need to break the bank to achieve them. If you're unable to invest your money, you can invest your time. Take your time to attain absolute consistency throughout your creative assets as this will evoke trust in your audience. There are some simple actions you can take to maintain a consistent brand image such as:

★ Record HEX codes for your colour palette

★ Create a library of on-brand imagery

★ Edit photos using the same "action" or filter

★ Select one to two fonts and commit to them

There are plenty of free options when selecting assets such as fonts or photography, however please ensure that your choices are royalty-free and that copyright extends to your usage. This is clearly explained and highlighted on reputable websites like Google Fonts and Unsplash (stock images).

Alternatively — if you're handy with a camera — you could capture your own brand photos. This way, you own the copyright and the only limitations are your skills and imagination. The library of on-brand imagery should set the tone for your brand so capture lifestyle images to inspire your audience. Don't forget to consider your brand colours! Avoid lots of product cameo shots at this stage… save them for e-commerce and product advertising.

Curate these guidelines using free tools like Canva or Google Doc (or, if you're feeling fancy, hire a designer) to begin your brand bible. This needs to be the go-to resource for you and your team so you can all be brand ambassadors and guardians.

Another way to craft your brand on a budget is through social media. Platforms like Facebook, Instagram, and X (formerly known as Twitter) are essentially free to use. Furthermore, they provide access to diverse audiences so you can promote your brand to the world and generate today's "word of mouth" buzz!

Always consider your tone of voice whenever you engage with audiences through comments or captions. With a few clever guidelines, you can draft your copy for free, and build a sense of community. It may feel easy to slip into your own way of writing (especially if your brand is closely linked with you) but you may not be your brand. Observe how your target customer communicates and mirror them to build rapport.

In addition to consistent tone of voice, you can apply consistent visual branding to your social media channels. Use the same colours through your content, banners and avatars, and develop your own iconic style of imagery.

There is an argument amongst marketers and gurus that you must invest in paid advertising, as the world of social media expands, in order to stay seen. It's a competitive place and channels will understandably prioritise the visibility of their big spenders. However, if paid advertising is not viable for your business, there are more affordable options.

Be patient and follow a regimented content marketing plan. This is the strategic scheduling and creation of videos or photos to visualise your brand experience. Many small businesses now use free tools like Canva or simply their smartphone's camera to create content for their business. For instance, a dog groomer can share adorable footage of a cockapoodle receiving a trim to express the personal and creative ethos of the company. Audiences love dogs and will feel a positive connection with the brand.

If you continue to share creative, purposeful content, and interact with your audience through meaningful comments, you can create a loyal following for your brand… for free!

## 7.9   EXPERIENCES

Brand experience is formed from the emotion and behavioural response when a customer interacts (directly or indirectly) with a specific brand. A range of experiences can be manufactured through a brand's website, print advertisements, social media account, packaging, physical stores and customer service (to name a few).

This experience holds a wealth of potential for businesses and should be considered carefully. Traditional advertising methods are losing favour with savvy customers who are craving unique engagement and connectivity. It is widely believed that if brands can scratch a customer's itch with unique experiences, they can connect on a more emotional level, and boost sales. Moreover, if a brand seal-the-deal with assured consistency and familiarity, they can build a loyal fanbase.

In the past, most companies focused on the physical aspects of products and services, such as price, functionality, quality, or availability. These aspects are easily replicable by competitors, and we know there is fierce competition in contemporary markets. Companies are expected to improve and evolve constantly to maintain their desired position. By differentiating your brand through exciting experiences, you can engage customers in a more meaningful relationship.

Brand experience is a no-brainer opportunity when marketing your business, but it is also your biggest challenge. How can you keep customers engaged when expectations of brands are increasing?

## 7.10 THE LITTLE THINGS MEAN A LOT

Attention to detail is essential because the lack of it is so evident to your clients and customers. It's the small gestures that provide a magical experience for your clients. Your audience can even pick up on the tiniest of signals.

Consider all parts of your customer journey to make a positive and long lasting impression. You may consider every aspect to enhance the ambience of a brand. From the tone of voice to the scent of your space, make your human encounters positive! It will help establish trust, and in turn, community.

The journey is imperative because it encourages exploration and moments of discovery. As human beings, we crave meaning and novelty in our quotidian routines. Shopping (for anything) can provide us with satisfaction if there is excitement within the process. We research online, and we hit the shops. There's excitement, inspiration and socialising. We browse, consider and strike! We part with our money, and at that moment, we feel in control. It satisfies our "hunter-gatherer" Neanderthal brain. If shopping becomes too automated, it loses this. Therefore, aim to surprise!

This proves how shopping (for products or services) has become an activity with a higher purpose. It is no longer a case of scavenging for survival. Instead of buying functional necessities, we search for inspiration and an unforgettable experience. We want to be stimulated and to be able to write home about it too. In an overloaded marketplace, you can use innovative experiences to gain a competitive edge.

It is why the lifestyle store has risen to fame. It encourages a journey of discovery through the narrative of a particular theme (such as wellbeing). It provides inspiration and knowledge, leaving the customer wanting more! It can be achieved online or offline, for product-based or service-based businesses.

When you provide a thought-out service to your customer, you show your dedication and pride in your brand! It's contagious and encourages your customers to feel the same way. They'll associate their time with you as delightful, recommending the brand to their friends and family too. Word-of-mouth, it's the best form of marketing!

Product or service, it's all in the delivery. Find ways to infuse authenticity, expertise and care in the delivery, so the experience benefits your customer. You can hone the skill of creating a rich brand experience. To achieve this, weave a narrative around all steps of the journey, from research to transaction to use. These touches give reasons for customers to dwell, further increasing their chances of making a purchase!

Whether you think of your website or physical store, treat it like a storybook. The homepage or facade is the dust jacket, and the content forms the paragraphs. Your customers twist and turn, on an adventure. When they make their purchase, they truly feel accomplished.

## 7.11 YOUR BRAND EXPERIENCE STRATEGY

With the presence of consumer giants, let's be real, sometimes you cannot compete with pride, scale and volume. Trust us, you don't need to! Instead focus on building an exceptional experience. If you can succeed in these following areas, you can attract and retain a loyal audience. Therefore, use these elements to create your plan of action:

★ Proficiency
★ Quality

★ Customer service
★ Social goodness

In this fickle, digital world, our attention span is shrinking, ghosting is normal behaviour, and we are addicted to technology. To cut through the commercial noise, you must be skilled at offering refreshing and relevant content to capture and keep attention. As well as captivating the eye, your product or service needs to be refined enough, so you are giving people what they want with ease. Your brand experiences must acknowledge this. Once this occurs, your customers feel understood and connected. You will need to execute a well-planned strategy across digital and offline platforms to communicate this.

Your brand is like a theatre. You have the opportunity to use your business as a stage; it is a platform to tell stories and connect on an emotional level. Break the fourth wall and share your world with the public. In theatre, actors and crew need to remain flexible and agile, as events unravel in real time — anything could happen! As brand builders, we need to be the same. Be open-minded to the possibilities. The strategy need not be a rigid "to-do" list. There may be times where improvisation is required. However, a well-thought-out brand provides a stable backdrop.

The following ideas can work for companies selling products or services, online or offline. Everything can be adapted to suit your needs and audiences. Trust us, it is easier when you have a strong brand strategy to guide you. Your brand guidelines become a toolkit for future campaigns and activations.

Could you try the following?

**Offline:**

★ Use props, creative staging to create contained scenes and themed displays.
★ Consider clever wayfinding or navigational tools to help your customers navigate through your store and direct them through the shopping experience.

★ Curate offerings into a limited but thoughtful selection or feature eye-grabbing abundance. Be confident in your choice. If you decide to offer only a couple of each product at any time, this can encourage joyful, serendipitous discovery!

★ Use lighting to create a memorable atmosphere within your physical space.

★ Physical stores should be places people want to spend time in, so make it welcoming! Think of introducing comfortable places to sit.

★ It sounds obvious, but ensure you welcome everyone and acknowledge those who interact with you. A small greeting can make a huge difference.

★ Offer your space as a meeting place where your audience can get involved and learn.

**Online:**

★ Allow for surprise discoveries as part of the customer journey. Your website and social media should be a destination, a playground of inspiration.

★ People are nosey, so reveal "behind the scenes" imagery and stories from your team to offer an insight into your process.

★ Make the most of your website's homepage. This is your book cover, and you are being judged (whether you like it or not)! If people don't like what they see, it's so easy to click off your site.

★ Facilitate a chat show or podcast to create more content to engage your audience. It gives you another reason to market yourself and encourages a sense of community.

★ Music can have a huge emotive impact on your audiences. Therefore, curate an uplifting, branded Spotify playlist.

You can use these ideas to introduce more magic to your brand. Try and captivate each of our five senses: touch, sight, hearing, smell and taste. Admittedly, it can be challenging as a digital organisation to introduce tangibility. However, if you can physically close the gap between you and your customer, they will feel more connected. Thank you notes, beautifully packaged mailers and personal meetings can help with this.

## ABIGAIL'S REFLECTION

❝ The Coronavirus Pandemic of 2020 shook our business and all we knew. We suddenly transitioned from a high-touch world to a low-touch world. The transformation was so quick, one Saturday we were performing live illustration with Seasalt Cornwall, and by Monday, lock-down commenced! How were we going to conduct similar interactive experiences now?

We created a new art performance in a virtual space which celebrated individuals and strengthened our community. Our virtual sessions were live-streamed to social media and saw us illustrate to an audience in real-time. We also provided weekly 'Branding Bites' where we provided practical guidance to support other small businesses.

It helped us fight social isolation, encourage inclusion and promote general wellbeing during the challenging period. Social media was the perfect tool for this. With platforms like Twitch, Facebook and YouTube, you can build relationships within a live environment. There can be a dialogue between watchers and the streamer. Participants can be active, social and impact the content as it's being created and delivered. Therefore, celebrating community and creativity (in an innovative way).

Experience is how you activate your brand and bring it to life. An array of special experiences will always draw audiences from across the globe. When you consider experience, you can create an attractive, multifaceted proposition, that your community will love and thank you for.

· · · · · · · · · · · · · · · · · ·

It's easy to imagine brand experience realised through consumer settings such as retail stores and restaurants. Think — atmospheric lighting, supersized advertisements, music, and delicious scents… Companies like Apple, Abercrombie & Fitch Co, and Lush are famous for their experiential spaces. Customers enter these stores and are transported to another world… another community.

You can utilise experiential design to cultivate a community in non-retail settings too. It's important that company offices captivate visitors, prospects, and talent, through thoughtful branding. Furthermore, a well-designed office can boost productivity amongst employees. An inspiring work environment will communicate a brand's respect for its staff while driving positive recruitment.

## CHLOE'S REFLECTION

❝ Take your time when scouting out your business' home and don't lose heart if the right space isn't immediately available. We launched Buttercrumble from our tiny spare room which we crammed with two desks and a bookcase.

We didn't realise how many times we'd be expected to answer "Where are you based?" and "Can I meet you at your office?" Our spare room couldn't cut the mustard and, after two years of awkward meetings in local coffee shops, we decided to sign for a professional office space.

We drafted a list of our needs (which included "no commute" and "natural light") and calculated our budget. This allowed us to shortlist an array of different offices which we viewed with an open-mind. We visited huge corporate office blocks, co-working spaces, and converted properties, before falling in love with a grade II listed building.

Brand experience is paramount to us. We want design partners to feel inspired when they walk into our studios. They see us as a safe pair of hands ready to deliver some sweet Buttercrumble results! Hence, we call ourselves the Happiness Atelier.

The building embodied this magic — but — there was no room at the inn! We had to continue our search for haven, just like Mary and Joseph, and settled on the next best thing. Now, don't get me wrong, our office was certainly not a stable! It ticked all our boxes… local, quirky, available parking, light and bright… and it was within budget.

We settled in our space for three pivotal years. We welcomed different team members, battled a global pandemic, and an economic crisis. You can see why — once our lease expired — we were ready for a change. The clock was ticking and, despite our best efforts, we couldn't find anything "Buttercrumble".

Then, at the final minute, the phone rang! Our dream office was calling.

Although the timing was unfortunate in 2019, the universe works in mysterious ways, we took our golden opportunity in 2022. Our new studio is a breath of fresh air and has definitely elevated our business. Our team is happier, the space is inspiring, and we're motivated for the future.

. . . . . . . . . . . . . . . . .

We've discussed the magic of brick-and-mortar, however, there's been a significant shift towards virtual workspaces. This was accelerated by the COVID-19 pandemic which forced many of us to work from home.

Businesses need to consider our post-COVID lifestyles. It's forecast that our neighbourhoods will become the magnet for life's events rather than be enticed by the city (which now feels somewhat risky). We'll work from home and travel shorter distances, opting for local grocers, charity shops, and independent coffee-shops. Our suburbs and districts are becoming sustainable spaces.

Food shortages and an increased cost of living has motivated consumers to become more self-sufficient. They've gained an appreciation of slow living, forced by recent lock-downs (WGSN, 2023).

Consequently, this has contributed to the demise of the high street. Empty shop units are beginning to convert into residential hubs with homes, care and leisure spaces. Brands are opening their eyes to the change, with John Lewis and IKEA planning to convert some spaces into private and social housing (Harper, 2020). However, we will still need physical retail spaces to provide consumers with tangible brand experiences and act as exciting and entertaining destinations.

Think about how you can take a local and sustainable approach to brand experiences. Support local makers and meet your community through small events. Could you situate your business in smaller neighbourhoods? Or do you even need a physical presence?

A plethora of businesses trade solely online via their website and social media. However, a new and immersive platform is on the horizon… cue, the Metaverse! Hmm…

It's promoted as a developed cyberspace, the new internet, and a virtual world. As the concept evolves, the only limit is your imagination, and it's important to be prepared for this new space. The Metaverse may offer a more seamless shopping experience to the online world today. Say goodbye to individual web pages and hello to a virtual mall.

Vast improvements need to be made to virtual reality and augmented reality equipment in order for consumers and brands to interact in the Metaverse. However, the concept has certainly sparked our imagination. As a business you need to stay up-to-date with market trends so you can provide relevant and innovative experiences to your consumer. Move with the times or risk being left behind!

## 7.12 WORKING WITH A DESIGNER

If you're ready to launch your brand with pizazz and aplomb, while saving your own valuable time, we recommend working with a designer. We may be a little biassed, as a creative agency, but design really is a worthwhile investment! It makes perfect economical sense to build a team of dedicated professionals as experts are scrupulous, expeditious, and purposeful. Pay someone who can outshine you on results and speed.

When considering a designer as an employee or contracted agency, pick someone who has relevant industry experience and shares your values. It can be tempting to select a versatile designer and, naturally, there's a strong case for all-rounders! However, a Jack of all trades is a master of none. You need to ensure that they, as a designer, can truly connect with your audience. Do they have the right specialisms to eradicate barriers to engagement and provide commercially-viable solutions?

You need to have a purposeful conversation with your shortlisted designers to determine whether you'll be a match made in heaven. Both parties need to listen carefully and communicate expectations as it takes two to tango. We appropriately titled this (in our own process) as the "listening" stage.

As a client, it's your opportunity to define the brief and to understand the designer's process. It's the designer's opportunity to learn as much as possible about your business, dreams, challenges, and target customer. Both sides need to ask questions — no matter how seemingly silly — to understand the task ahead. A partnership between client and designer is a meaningful commitment which shouldn't be taken lightly.

You can guarantee a similar collaboration process from agency to agency although we recognise everyone has unique-selling-points and foibles. Our process is as follows:

**Listen:** We are approached with a creative project or problem. We take the time to understand our design partners' unique needs through email, face-to-face meeting, or a phone call. We ask questions and offer initial suggestions so we can be confident about our offered solution.

**Agreement:** Together, we'll define the brief in our standard terms and conditions document. This outlines the commitment including payment terms, schedules, delivery dates, and transference of usage rights. It's important that the agreement benefits both parties so ensure you take the time to carefully consider the proposed agreement.

**Discovery:** Once an agreement has been reached we can evolve the creative plan and strategy for the project. We may hold further discussions with our design partner or conduct independent research to ensure we present fitting recommendations and initial concept visuals.

**Creative:** We develop the approved concept to produce and present a confident solution. Our design partner receives a visual solution and strategy with clear direction. We are dedicated to creating an outcome which solves your business challenges.

**Refine:** We're passionate about collaboration and regular feedback sessions allow everyone to feel invested in the solution! Each opportunity for feedback is clearly communicated in our terms and agreement so the project can stay on-track for success.

**Delivery:** At the end of the project, before delivery, the work is reviewed to our exacting standard. We like to build long-term relationships with our design partners so they know we're there for them moving forward. We revel in our partners' success which is why we work collaboratively on a plan so they can take true ownership of their new designs.

This process is best suited for projects with a clear timeframe and end deliverable. However, we appreciate that some design partners require more flexible support to develop brand campaigns or new products. This is why we offer an open-access support service. You may also hear this referred to as a "retainer". This is where the client will invest every month for a fixed amount of consultancy and design time from their agency. The benefits of this model are that the client has peace of mind knowing that they have time dedicated to their needs every month, there's no fluctuating investment, clients can receive unlimited revisions within your monthly allowance, and they are treated as a priority.

## 7.13 HOW TO WRITE A DESIGN BRIEF

You'll need a considered design brief before you and your designer can get cracking on beautiful deliverables. These clear expectations can be communicated before engagement with an agency or a brief may be created in collaboration with the appointed design team.

A good design brief must outline specific aims and objectives; it sets the tone for a successful project. The details can take some time to iron out but it's worth it! It will help maintain the quality, budget, and schedule as both parties will feel fully involved in the process.

Ensure your brief covers a brand overview, aims and objectives, target audience, budget, timeline, and deliverables. As a helpful guide, you could answer the following questions:

- ★ What does your company do, and how is it unique?
- ★ Do you have brand guidelines?
- ★ What's your company's mission?
- ★ Are you facing any roadblocks or challenges as a business?
- ★ What are your primary design needs?
- ★ What will make this a successful project?

★ How do you measure success?

★ Who is your target audience and how does your company help them?

★ When do you expect to receive the final deliverables?

★ What is the project budget?

★ How quickly can you deliver feedback?

★ What is your preferred method of delivering feedback?

★ Who are the company's competitors?

★ Which brands do you aspire to?

★ What are the deliverables for this project?

Vague briefs can lead to scope-creep and, in turn, additional investment or delays. Defined expectations are useful for the designer to determine the project's scope. As a result, everyone can keep on-track without hidden surprises.

^      *Stratford Together. We created this campaign in collaboration with a place-making expert from Stratford Original BID. Residents were able to pledge acts of kindness over the festive period and share how they were helping their community members. We implemented the campaign across digital and print.*

*It all started with a sketch and concepts. Stratford is a characterful town in East London, and we wanted to celebrate the people who live there.*

^     *Campaign illustrations for Mamas & Papas*

*Chapter 8*

# TRACKING AND PIVOTING

*"You got to know when to hold
'em, know when to fold 'em..."*
*– Kenny Rogers*

The elephant in the room can often be money. However, without turnover and profit, businesses would cease to exist, you need to ensure your business can make a living. If you hit a sticky point on your business journey, you may need to pivot your brand. By re-establishing brand desire, you can boost profits, simply through nurturing trust and connection. You need to be transparent with your audience.

In times of crisis, innovation is vital. For example, LEGO credits its success to its ability to keep focus during difficult times. They strive and survive because it lays the path for the future. In the words of LEGO's (former Vice President) Connie Kalcher — "the companies that are really successful in innovation are the companies that realise that innovation comes from everywhere, from all employees, no matter what they do" (Leader Lab. 2010). Yet, don't feel like you need to reinvent the wheel. Innovation is not just about creating new things — it's improving customer value. It can include all aspects of a business. It's a cumulative effort to improve your company. It will help keep it alive and kicking!

Business innovation and marketing professors from Northwestern University (Sawhney et al., I. 2007) have outlined a range of ways your organisation can innovate and lengthen the life of your organisation:

★ Network for knowledge and opportunities.
★ Redefine the ways your company gets paid by creating new revenue streams.
★ Redesign your core operating processes to improve efficiency.
★ Diversify your company's activities. For example, you could introduce a new social-good initiative.
★ Think differently about sourcing to create a new point of difference.
★ Create new points of presence for your brand.
★ Catapult your brand into new realms by creating an alluring lifestyle around your product or service.
★ Develop derivative offerings, building upon your current offerings. Allow customers to pick and mix!
★ Create customised services and products.
★ Discover your customer's unmet needs.
★ Redesign interactions across all touchpoints.
★ Be prepared to create new products or services when your audience's needs change.

With this list of ideas, your company doesn't have an excuse for becoming obsolete! When it's time to pivot, consider the above.

## CHLOE'S REFLECTION

❝ When starting a business, you'll meet people who will (undoubtedly) have an opinion on your venture. To be frank, it's none of their business!

I remember arriving at an event at the top of an office block in Leeds, as I emerged from the dinghy lift, I was swiftly handed a beer token. The usher ushered me into a huge open-plan industrial space. The event was advertised as a support network for creatives and this covered industry old-hands, freelancers, and students. The set-up of the room felt like a boxing ring. The expert support set-up in one corner and the rest of us, in the other. People were scattered around the edges of the room, and I remember a distinct lack of collaboration in the air. I find this to be a common result when throwing a handful of introverted artists, academics, and designers together.

Nonetheless, I was paired with a member of the Spanish Inquisition who quizzed me on our business. With a few taps on her laptop, she had pulled up Buttercrumble and suggested a rebrand. In her eyes, the name was too silly, and we needed our social media links placed in the primary navigation bar. She felt the colour pink would be too feminine and, in turn, would repel male clients. "Well," I said, "most of our clients are men". It is a modern world, after all.

Not only this, but we also received advice through a graduate award. And, despite being advocates for creativity, our advisors also suggested an alternative to the name "Buttercrumble". Their recommendation was fairly conservative and straight-to-the-point. "How about, Abigail and Chloe Baldwin?" They probed."Well," I said again "it's not about us". And, the name Buttercrumble remained.

. . . . . . . . . . . . . . . . . .

Another time, a businessman confronted us at an event of ours. He explained how he'd heard so much about us, could see our success on social media, but just had to see us for himself! I believe the online world — especially social media — has created scepticism. You can paint a tailored image to display yourself favourably. Naturally, we always try to show Buttercrumble in the best light. Hence, the man concluded that the hype was real. He was blown away by our nature. Maybe it's because we're Yorkshire Lasses and we call a spade a spade, but many have commented on our genuineness. We bring our personal values into our business, and one of those is to be yourself!

Another man confronted us at an illustration event (we can't get away from it) and exclaimed: "I knew it was you, straight away!" By curating a transparent image on social media, we've become approachable, and instantly recognisable. Don't be nervous portraying the real, authentic you. Everyone is unique, and we can use our foibles to our advantage.

We may sound stubborn, but we do acknowledge that not everything is a success. We evaluate and monitor our decisions so we know when to make a change. When winning is presented as the only option within the business world (and often society), quitting may feel like the end of the world. Use your honest instinct to know whether your business needs to pivot or bow-out.

## 8.1 IN TIMES OF TROUBLE

If a year was to win an award for "Top Pivoter" it would be 2020. It was a transformative year for everyone as we incorporated new ways of living. The coronavirus pandemic is arguably "the biggest global driver of change" in recent history according to a WGSN report (2020, p.2). The crisis stopped many businesses in their tracks (including us) and many had to rethink their business models. The isolation during the crisis took us back in time to our early days. We started the business remotely, in front of our computers, and we were forced to return due to the lock-down. It made many businesses rethink their overheads regarding office space and encouraged digital collaboration and innovative services. Gifts can be found in the darkest of places.

We regularly reminded ourselves that lock-down could not last forever, but we knew the world had changed permanently due to the tragedy of the virus. It is an upsetting thought as, although we are surviving through digital connectivity, we are craving a human connection.

WGSN also heralded 2020 as "the dawn of the connected decade" (2020, p.3). They forecast that by 2022, the majority of our world would connect through 5G and internet technology. The world can communicate and receive news in real-time. We will not only be connected digitally — but emotionally too. Feelings and reactions towards major events will transmit on a global scale.

Buttercrumble falls into the profile "The Settlers" as described by WGSN. Funnily enough, the group typically comprises Millennials. We are here to innovate while strengthening the ties in our community. We are not here to settle but to nurture our local community and embrace spontaneity. We appreciate the sentiment of 'equitable resilience' and are ready to accept the uncertainty. Resilience is a key trait of business owners and entrepreneurs. After all, this isn't the first time we've had to adapt, and it certainly won't be the last.

While there is a growing trend towards resilience and, in Britain, haven't we always had a stiff upper lip? We must be aware of the dangers surrounding grit. Sometimes you have to accept when it's time to stop for wellbeing's sake.

When we continue to consider WGSN's research, we predict our client base will fall into the profile "The New Optimists" thanks to their appetite for joy. This broad audience — young and old — want to push through the negative. They know progress is being made in the world and they want to dismiss the fear-mongering media. In order to reach this audience, we must utilise the power of the pack, and nurture our Crumble Club. In times of trouble, the community comes together.

Buttercrumble is fortunate because so many of our services are delivered digitally. Our live illustration events took a hit but we found ways to give workshops using video technology. We partnered with the Business and IP Centre and The Old Bank Residence (NOMA) to share our guidance and support free-of-charge.

With a national lock-down in place, restaurants adapted to the situation by boosting their delivery offering, and e-commerce companies like Amazon reaped the rewards. Gyms and classes pivoted their business by providing fitness sessions via video-link.

## *8.2* STICK OR TWIST

Now, it is essential to listen to the feedback of others. We are advocates of the pivot, of course. However, it is also right to figure out when to stick rather than twist. It is something we have had to learn throughout our business' lifetime.

On the other hand, sticking with your brand can bring benefits (if you strategise well). The age of your brand can increase brand equity, but many business managers swap and hesitate more times than they change their underwear. If your branding is always "umm"-ing and "ahh"-ing, your audience is going to be left feeling confused. Try not to blow hot and cold with your customers! They'll move on to the next best thing.

The strongest brands have been clear, consistent and persistent over a long time. McDonald's, Coca-Cola and even Marmite. They've stuck with their identity for decades. Instead, they alter the messaging of their advertising campaigns, whilst still staying true to the core brand values. This is key. Organisations should have multiple (yet well-aligned values). Different campaigns can focus on each of these depending on the current climate.

Yet, we like to change. The main reasons for an organisational re-brand are ownership, trends, and boredom.

**Ownership:** this is a reason for change when there is a new leader or manager within an organisation. They want to put their stamp on the company, so they feel an identity shake-up will help them succeed. It's a clear and visible change which indicates to the rest of the team that they have achieved something. They now feel fully integrated within their place of employment.

**Trends:** just like fashion, branding alters to trends. From rainbows to fidget spinners, we've had some crazy fads over the last decade. However, just because "keep calm and carry on" motifs are popular, doesn't mean we need to incorporate them into a brand identity. Trends are often short-lived, don't allow your organisation to fall into this trap. Stay true to your brand's style and always refer back to your core values.

**Boredom:** you may have been staring at the same set of values on your office wall for the last three years. You're bored of them and the logo. It's everywhere you look when you're at work. It's OK — this is a natural feeling. However, your customers don't feel the same way. They are not exposed to your brand nearly as much as you are. Instead, see it as comforting familiarity.

If it ain't broke, don't fix it.

## CHLOE'S REFLECTION

66 Buttercrumble has opened up the most wonderful network of people to us. It's always an inspiration to hear about other business journeys and each one is different. We believe

in uplifting and supporting others because the road is difficult. Even before launching Buttercrumble, we would support businesses.

Whilst working at her digital marketing agency, Abigail met a creative entrepreneur who had seen great success. Their kindness and enthusiasm were welcomed by Abigail and the relationship was founded. We both followed him along the journey and — at times — it was difficult to see the struggles and setbacks they faced. He was forced to pivot which was ultimately a stroke of genius. Yet, the vital gamification aspect of his business (its heart) was kept. He went from renting a desk in a small office to owning a large office in central Leeds. The business even appeared on television so it's well-known in Leeds and beyond. Whenever we bump into each other, we always have a friendly natter, we're so pleased to see how the business has helped his family. It's a real joy and pleasure when we get to work together, he's hosted several panels we've appeared on.

Every business story unfolds at different speeds. Yes, we've seen some people find big success after a few years, and some people are still where they set off. We continue to support a friend with business ambitions but they have barely taken two steps since their announcement three years ago. They have researched, evaluated, interviewed, planned and modelled their business to the minutest detail. Have they made a sale? No. Will they ever launch their business? We are beginning to wonder. After a couple of years, I began to wonder why they hadn't leapt yet.

After all, we can resemble a dog with a bone. When we experience a eureka moment, we propel ourselves forward, keeping our focus on the ultimate goal. When you operate your own business, you hold the reins of your destiny!

I state this without underestimating the true challenges of running a business. We maintain the mindset that to ignore pain is to ignore our potential. Pain is an integral part of life's rich tapestry, and without mistakes, we cannot acquire knowledge and evolve. The setbacks may be agonising, yet they also bring us one step closer to our intended destination.

When I look at our bank balance and see every hard-earned penny, I can sleep easy at night, knowing I deserve financial success. When we receive a thank you card from our client, I know the tears and long nights were worth it. When I can get up each morning to work alongside my twin sister, I know we're on the right path.

I think our friend's lack of get-up-and-go is due to a fear of failure but they should fear the opportunity that is passing them by. We regret the things we didn't do.

. . . . . . . . . . . . . . . . . .

## 8.3   CAST YOUR NET WIDER

In May 2022, we completed our first international business trip as a team of three. We travelled to the US where we nurtured our client relationships and expanded our minds.

From the moment we touched down in New York, we were met with excitement. The taxi stand conductor — a petite blonde lady — hurled orders to the drivers in a thick New York accent. Once we were in our taxi we were surrounded by gangs of kids on dirt bikes and trikes, performing wheelies and tricks, like rodeo cowboys. They wore military style helmets and dominated the road.

Despite their tough-talking reputation, the New Yorkers were surprisingly kind to us! We love the open nature of Americans. We received so many lovely compliments on our British style from complete strangers. It included the co-working boss, hotel guests, and our new friends, Carley-Anne and Belle from Utah. They stopped us in Times Square en route to an advertising awards ceremony.

We were mesmerised by Ellen's Stardust Diner where adorable waitresses wearing bunches and pink glasses would jump onto the furniture and break out in Broadway numbers. The gritty glamour continued on the subway where we saw the most immaculate drag queen. The mix of razzle-dazzle and urbanism offered generous creative inspiration.

Our first client meeting was set at The Whitby Bar, off Madison Avenue, close to Tiffany & Co. We were attracted to the name of the location due to our connections with Whitby on the east coast of England. The decor, amusingly, did not have a nautical theme. Nonetheless, we were bowled over by the designs which we later discovered were the work of Kit Kemp. Everything was served with total aplomb and when Shawn walked in... we were enthralled. We got on like a house on fire and we were thrilled to meet his wife too. Verona was immaculately presented in a LBD, pearl earrings, and silk scrunchie — true Audrey Hepburn style.

Our second meeting was in a swanky hotel lobby with one of our treasured, long-standing clients. We were reuniting, after working remotely for four years, and the anticipation was immense. It was a proud moment to introduce our newest team member to our client. After all, they supported us from our early days and have witnessed our growth. More gifts were exchanged and it was refreshing to brainstorm ideas face-to-face.

The department stores proved inspiring. Retail is a second-level in the US. It's perhaps one area where the Americans have the innovation edge. In Nordstrom, the customer assistant presented a mini-me outfit from the kids section. They'd taken the time to analyse Chloe's outfit and picked out a miniature version. This personalised service was reflected through personalisation stations too. You can get any item customised through appliqué, painting, embroidery, and engraving.

The conference offered plenty of food for thought too. We listened to a full schedule of trend insights and future forecasts. It left us wondering… What does the future hold? This new perspective helped to revitalise our business and filled us with energy.

Our perspectives were widening, but the world felt smaller. We were amused to meet a fellow Brit, living locally to us, at an international conference. She worked for a major telecommunications company in the UK, and she even sat next to us on the plane home!

Despite all the excitement and inspiration, we felt a huge blow on returning from our first team US trip. In a matter of days, our only employee resigned with new-found plans. We were shocked and upset as the news felt so unexpected. We have always known and understood that team members eventually move on, but we didn't expect to hear a resignation immediately after our trip... We had such a wonderful time. The news has left us under a rain cloud and — in spite of our inspiring trip — we needed to re-spark our motivation.

Where there is dark, light can be found. We all worked so hard on our business trip so we held hope. We were ready to reap what we sowed and our prayers didn't let us down. Our meetings in the Big Apple were certainly fruitful as we were rewarded with new projects — what a win! There is an expense (monetary and energy) with international travel. But, it's totally worth it. We are enriched with beautiful memories and meaningful connections.

This positive thought propelled us on our second trip to New York which came only a few months later. We were eager to build on the valuable connections we made in May-time and arranged further follow-up meetings with our clients. Exporting does require additional effort in order to build business connections and these relationships should not be taken for granted.

We attended a trade show with the aim of connecting with 25 exhibitors. It was our chance to make personal introductions and promote our creative services, but we knew it wouldn't be an easy sell. After all, exhibitors are trying to use their valuable time to sell to buyers and distributors.

The first brand we approached immediately turned away on our introduction — eh-oh! It was tough to receive a face-to-face rejection, but we wouldn't be deterred. We looked at each other, gave an encouraging nod, and tapped the representative on the shoulder. "Excuse me, we really love your brand and we'd love to feature you!" We had piqued their interest and we were on a roll!

**Our tips for international travel:**

★ Set goals and have a backup plan. A business trip can be hugely rewarding, but it's no holiday. You need to have goals in place to benefit your business and make your trip worthwhile. A clear plan that allows for quick adaptation is essential.

★ Avoid layovers. All our business flights (including a 13-hour flight from Hong Kong) have been non-stop. These flights can feel arduous, but layovers lengthen trips. It might not be necessary to spend an extra day on the road or risk lost luggage in transfer.

★ Print important information. It's so easy to rely on our digital devices in this day-and-age. However, it can be helpful to print any important information for quick, safe access.

★ Pack healthy snacks and breakfast. You need to be on top form when you're jet-setting, networking, and negotiating. Pack some convenient (but healthy) food to help you stay well while travelling. We champion ready-to-go porridge pots for breakfast as an easy way to save money and time.

★ Keep an essentials bag. If you travel regularly, it's a good idea to pack a separate bag with toiletries, chargers, business cards, and stationery. Store your essentials bag safely, on your return, for quick access on your next trip.

★ Be prepared for airport security. Don't be that person holding up queues in security! Airport protocols are easy-to-find so you can be prepared for every visit. Store your liquids and electronics in an easily accessible place. Consider your footwear and accessories carefully as you may be required to remove these.

★ Prioritise sleep. It can be difficult to catch your rest when travelling. Make your life easier by packing noise-cancelling headphones or earbuds, and an eye mask.

★ Collect receipts. Get in the habit of requesting your receipts. These records are essential to track your expenses. Consider expense-tracking apps, if your bag is cluttered with paperwork, to store digital versions of your receipts.

## 8.4  TRANSFORMATION

### ABIGAIL'S REFLECTION

It did take a few tries to nail our current Buttercrumble brand down. At the time of creating our first logo, we were laymen! It featured an illustration of our mascot, Buttercrumble bear and a signature. It was personal and conveyed character. Our first brand colour was purple and I'm not even sure why. Yet, the execution could have been better! OK, we could have put a little more thought into it, but we were fresh-faced and eager. However, it didn't ooze enough professionalism! It wasn't setting the right expectations.

The second edition was much closer to what we have today. We introduced our berry tones and the love heart. The only problem was that "butter" and "crumble" were on separate lines. This confused our audience, as different written versions of our name appeared. We'd constantly have to correct "Butter Crumble". It's one word — not two. These lessons were important and helped us design for others.

We developed each identity, paying attention to what was harming our reputation. Your appearance, messaging and actions all affect the way others see you. This is your brand perception. If you know how you'd like to be perceived, you can work on your identity and marketing to achieve this. At Buttercrumble, we knew we wanted to be seen as professional with a creative twist. We wanted to embrace our youthfulness too. This led to the third incarnation and what you can see today. We've adopted this for at least four years now to build upon our brand equity.

. . . . . . . . . . . . . . . . . .

Brand equity is the value that derives from customer perception rather than the services or products of an organisation. Recognition plays a huge role in encouraging customers to invest. After all, they need to be aware of the brand first! Customers need to have experienced the brand in some shape or form before committing to it. If you are frequently changing your image, recall is difficult for the audience and you send out a vote of no confidence for your organisation. Think about it — if you don't believe in yourself, who else will? By keeping a consistent identity, you can build trust. Customers know they can rely on you without the onset of surprise. They know what they're getting, so feel secure in their investment. The relationship then continues to blossom. With customer resonance, you'll create brand ambassadors.

That's why we made the conscious decision to stay true to our current identity for as long as possible. Of course, you must pivot and be flexible to the needs of the evolving marketplace, but it needn't be a complete overhaul. Be like a palm tree — when the wind blows, you bend without breaking. The turbulence helps strengthen your roots. You grow stronger over time through small changes. You'll appear calm and reassuring to your audience.

Your visual identity is the flag you fly within the competitive marketplace. Flags were first used as field signs in combat and were even shown on clothing. They enabled friends, foes and civilians to be quickly recognised. Each group had a clear battle-cry and a fiery passion. They truly believed in something and weren't afraid to show it.

Although times have changed, it's still important you can fly the flag for your company. We are not suggesting you march into combat, instead, be driven, strategic and soulful. When you combine your identity with consistent communication, you can carve out a space for your tribe within the business landscape. Your brand possesses the power to recruit, connect consumers and even disarm your competitors. Business owners want to cultivate this ability and everyone can achieve this through thoughtful design.

As brand builders or company directors, you may be able to relate with the battlefield nature of business. Everything we've done in our lives has amounted to this moment within our careers. For us, there's a lot of stake. There was the labour of education, the fear of starting and the toil of growing. It's our livelihood so we have to be impassioned. Of course, we love it though. We are the proud flag-bearers, promoting all we believe in. Let us hear your battle cry.

When you start building a brand, you ask yourselves: "who are we?" This can be a challenging question to answer. You need to take the journey of self-awareness for your business. When we fully acknowledge who our organisation is (as a brand) and discover our core, we can be honest and open with customers. Your audience will feel seen and heard (and so will you).

What do you love? What are you afraid of? What inspires you? By contemplating the answers to these questions, you can explore your brand's core and stay consistent. Further building upon your brand equity.

At the core of Buttercrumble, we are an organisation that loves stretching the imagination. We want to empower young-at-heart businesses to express themselves visually. Moreover, our overall goal is to be creating smile-provoking work every day. There was a time where we were afraid of talking to other business owners through our insecurities, so we understand what it feels like to lack a way of expression. We are driven by the confidence helping others can bring and inspired by those we help. We are happiest when we are making ourselves smile, clients smile and customers smile too. This is all at our heart.

On the other hand, we notice when we are misaligned from our core as we make a habit of evaluating our brand regularly. We're disappointed when we struggle to transfer our exact vision from mind to paper. However, through persevering, we believe we can continue to grow stronger, wiser and better. We wish we could reveal the promise of progression to our younger selves and we wholeheartedly believe that Buttercrumble is a creative movement that will inspire other business owners every day.

When it comes to implementation, focus is the hero of the day. Focus is ultimately what will help you gain brand equity when it's practised over a long time. Focus is having the strength to say "no" and to ignore distractions. It's easy to be seduced by the trends and want to incorporate a new edgy angle. However, it may be leading you down a path which is eventually harmful for your company. You lose sight of what you are and it leaves your audience feeling disenchanted and disconnected. Whenever implementing any part of your brand, double-check it against your values and brand guidelines.

Even freelancers should consider their brand identity to communicate their personality and values to elevate themselves above competitors and demonstrate meaningful transformation. Freelancers often exchange time for money, so of course they are busy! With a thoughtful brand in place, it will do a huge amount of marketing for you without you needing to be there 24/7. It makes sense to hire your silent salesmen — branding.

After nearly ten years of working under the name of Buttercrumble, we are amassing quite the archive! I was recently clearing out some boxes at home and discovered the book we created around 2011. The book's design is shocking, but drove it home to me about how much we wanted the business to work as sixteen-year-olds.

I realise that we have been one of the fortunate ones. We've grown up knowing what we wanted to do with our lives, so it never feels too much like work. I knew there was no other option. Being creative was something I needed to do and if I wasn't, I'd drive myself crazy. This is it. Transformation is how a caterpillar morphs into a beautiful butterfly. What would feel like a victorious evolution to you and your business?

## 8.5   ON SET BACKS

We all know it's not all rainbows and butterflies in business! Chances are, you feel
overworked. As a solopreneur or business owner, you're constantly balancing your
family-life and work. Your health often takes a back-seat and this has been our experience
on so many occasions. From economic recessions to hiring and firing, from chasing debtors
to lengthy tenders, business can be stressful.

### ABIGAIL'S REFLECTION

**❝** Three months into the COVID-19 crisis, it was making us feel uneasy. I had
personally spent years cultivating a mindful approach to my work, I practised meditation,
and built a supportive network. This empowered me to keep a clear vision when
conducting business. I began to wonder if this had slipped out of place due to an intense,
unsettling feeling in the pit of my stomach. Practising self-care and nurturing your mental
health is essential as a business-owner. When you're steering the ship you have to protect
your physical and mental wellbeing to reduce time away. The importance of wellbeing was
felt more than ever during the crisis.

We are lucky as a twin-team. Our relationship is close and we can guide each other
through the hardships (whilst celebrating the good times)! It helps to acknowledge
the challenge to someone, and in turn, ourselves. Running a business is hard! You
are climbing a steep mountain that many chose to divert. It's not exactly a walk in
the park, so why do we beat ourselves up over the set-backs? Furthermore, we don't
start climbing that mountain with top-notch biz-boss gear... no, no, no. There is
no starter-pack to business success, you have to learn along the way, and build your
experience. We're never fully equipped to run a business. And, guess what, it's not
just you! The hardship is real and affects us all. The set-backs are not unique to your
circumstance, we all have to pick ourselves up, and dust our knees down. If you can
acknowledge all of this, you are showing yourself a bit of compassion.

You're compassionate and you can take a break. It's important to take time to play to
avoid major burn-out. The best ideas come to us when we're experimenting and allowing

ourselves to be creative. If you are working 24/7, you are leaving no headspace for the imagination. I have recently been reintroduced to the wonder of video games and I'm letting my inner-child shine through. If that's not your style, take your dog out for a walk or play board games with your family.

We are huge advocates for sleep too. It's an underrated basic human need. It can heal, renew, and rejuvenate you better than any magic pill or super juice. Yet so many of us are deprived of sleep and we wear our dark circles like a badge of honour. People boast that they can function with four hours of sleep per night, before waking up at 5am to go jogging before their school-run and networking session. We live in a society where people are striving to out-do each other, promote their "best lives" on Instagram, whilst running a six-figure business. This is madness. The truth is that life is messy, hard work, and tiring! When it gets to 9pm, we can't wait to be in our jim-jams (pyjamas) tucked up in bed. Of course, 7-9 hours a night isn't always possible but we should make sleep an essential part of our schedule. You will feel bright-eyed, bushy-tailed, and ready to take on the world.

. . . . . . . . . . . . . . . . . .

We thought COVID-19 would be the biggest challenge Buttercrumble would face so we knuckled down, pulled our socks up, and took bold risks.

This tactic can clearly bring results because a risk preceded each stage of our growth. The first risk? Abigail left her full-time job. The second risk? Chloe left her full-time job. The third risk? We invested in a studio space which gave us credibility. You get the idea… Buttercrumble grew. We hired team members. Buttercrumble grew. We engaged with external experts. Buttercrumble grew. These risks enabled our turnover to increase by 110% over the first three years.

However, the subsequent economic downturn of 2022 rippled through our business and caused major fractures. This led to sleepless nights and difficult decisions, but you have to be ready to face whatever life throws at you.

In addition to external factors, your inner demons sure can bite. Catastrophizing (blowing things out of proportion), jumping to conclusions, and blaming are unhelpful thinking styles. Though, unlike the global economy, there is an accessible antidote. It's time to be kinder to yourself.

Now, you don't necessarily need to go overboard and have a rehaul. Moderation is key to joy, and life can be about finding balance. There's tension between work and play. You have to consider when you act with discipline or exercise freedom. Sometimes you need friends around, and sometimes solitude. There is always movement and shifts in life's energy.

Think: are you more concerned with evolving as an individual or being right? It's good to have room for development, and you mustn't let your ego get in the way of this. Have an open heart to the opportunities ahead.

You can nurture this openness with a few different daily habits — find what works for you. We find the following activities super useful for staying strong during setbacks:

- ★ Write daily in a journal and express your gratitude for the little things.
- ★ Detox from social media and unplug!
- ★ Enjoy coffee and cake with a close friend or family member.
- ★ Stretch — yoga practice is a huge help.
- ★ Take a hot bath or shower, and you'll feel refreshed.

Overall, when pursuing your mission and vision, there are going to be bumps in the road. If you have a positive outlook, your resilience will be reinforced! We understand motivation is not always accessible, so you must learn to be disciplined. This is where having these thought-out plans comes into play. Be persistent.

A river cuts through a rock not because of its power, but its persistence.

^        *Let's Plate brand and packaging design*

# Chapter 9

# CONCLUSION

*Stay curious.*

———————————

When you are running a business, every day is so jam-packed. Your mind is bubbling with thoughts, so you have to take each moment as it comes. The speed of life is incredible, so it can be challenging to process everything.

Therefore, branding is always important for businesses and their teams. It becomes embedded, like DNA, running through everything. It becomes the intuition and guiding compass. As a founder, manager or whatever role you play, the branding becomes a feeling in your heart. You instinctively know what is right or wrong for the organisation.

It is this instinct that is critical when running a fast-paced business. So, do yourself a favour and hone your branding!

We believe branding can lead to confidence because it gives you an outlet for storytelling. You can be seen, heard and understood. This yearning for stories has been within us since the dawn of communication as it helps us interact and connect with others.

# The Brand Power Manifesto

## USE YOUR PERIPHERAL VISION 1

## ◎ 2 make it POWERFUL

you are the key to branding brilliance. Keep going. We believe in you.

(obviously!)

168

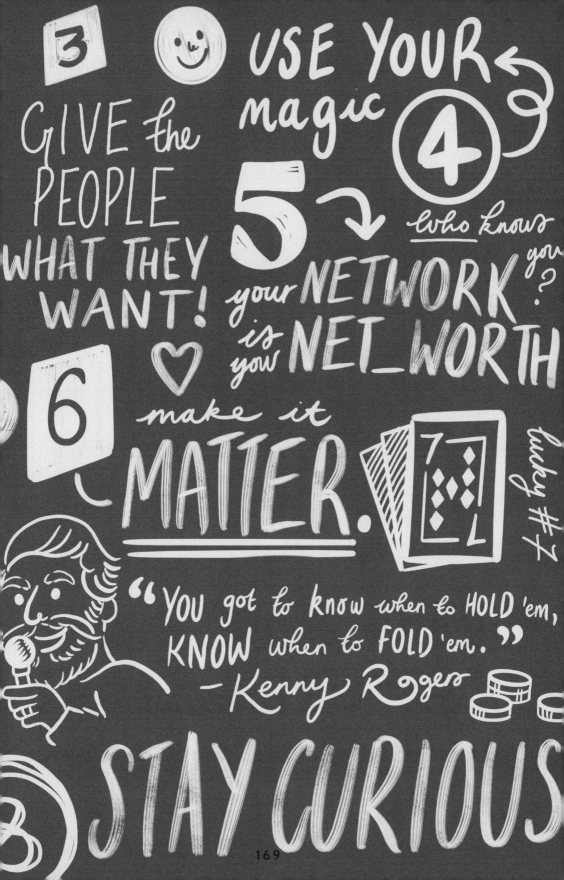

3 USE YOUR magic 4

GIVE the PEOPLE WHAT THEY WANT!

5 who knows you?

your NETWORK is your NET_WORTH

6 make it MATTER.

7 lucky #7

"YOU got to know when to HOLD 'em, KNOW when to FOLD 'em." - Kenny Rogers

STAY CURIOUS

The branding exercises shown within this will have helped you to explore your mission and vision. Keep in mind: what you yearn for, what you dislike, what you aspire to, and what you fear. You can express these in the form of memorable and powerful stories.

Tell your story, and share it with the world with branding as your platform. This has the power to unite your values and visions with people, everywhere. It acts as glue that binds us together as human beings. It creates loving and loyal communities.

Essentially, branding is the framework (or blueprint) for your business' heart and soul. Personality and language are complex, so use branding as a way to make sense of it for yourself and your team. After all, it takes a village to raise a child and an organisation to raise a brand!

We frequently host consultancy sessions and workshops for start-ups in partnership with the Business & IP Centre (part of the British Library). One participant mentioned: "when you apply branding to your business, it's that first moment when you know it's real. This really can be a "thing"!" It is an exciting hurdle for any start-up to jump.

Other people can see how much you care, so they want to support you too. Support breeds confidence, so it becomes a positive cycle — as long as you keep an eye on your future vision. Always keep dreaming.

We hope you can gain the same confidence we benefited from when developing our brand. By having your clear strategy, you can gain clarity in all aspects of your business. Most of all, it aids your marketing, so you feel proud of what you've nurtured and accomplished.

Finally, we are here for those who have ever had a dream (no matter its size). When you're caught up in real-time, you don't always respect or understand a moment's gravitas. It is why reflection is crucial. We hope this book has carved out time for you to do just that — reflect and build.

^ *Thanks so much for reading, with love from Abigail and Chloe*

1. Use your peripheral vision: An insight into strategic brand analysis
2. Make it powerful: Find the core of your brand
3. Give the people what they want: Communicate your unique value proposition
4. Use your magic: Gain credibility and be taken seriously
5. Your network is your net worth: Nurture relationships and build community
6. Make it matter: Implement what you've learnt
7. You got to know when to hold 'em, know when to fold 'em: Track and pivot to stay relevant
8. Stay curious: Keep looking to the future

## *9.1* OUR STATEMENT

When it comes to branding and business, we're always preaching the "why?" Why do we do what we do? We've always loved being creative by unravelling our minds with ink onto paper. When we were younger, we took this skill for granted, but then we matured. It can be frustrating for those who struggle to make use of a blank piece of paper. Especially when their mind is so excited about their vision. There's so many thoughts bubbling, it feels like their head may burst! That's where we step in. We help businesses express themselves, and in turn, connect with their audiences.

Our aspiration is to establish Buttercrumble as a globally respected creative studio for family audiences and community-sensitive brands. As we feel these are the organisations that intrinsically have people at the heart of what they do. Plus, they're always game for a bit of play.

Buttercrumble's holistic and transparent approach means the businesses we partner with are key to the success of the collaboration. They are taken along for the ride!

We always enjoy beginning the process with pencil sketching to create rough "scamps" before moving onto a computer. In the creative industries, a scamp is a rough sketch — ideas in their purest form. This foundation of trusty tradition aids our use of digital media.

Digital design allows us to work collaboratively across the world, which is why most designers adopt technology. After all, it's the modern age! It allows us to present popping colours, as well as multiple drafts without having to erase everything and start again.

The best part of our role is when we see a brand making an impact in the physical world. When we walk past a window display we created, it gives us a kick. When we see customers enjoying the display, it makes the whole process worthwhile. We've allowed that business to connect on an emotional level with the customer.

We know a design has turned out well when it sings. You look at it, and it feels harmonious. So much so, you want to continue appreciating its form and colours. This occurs when all the different elements are working peacefully and efficiently together within one piece — like a well-oiled machine, but arty.

Currently, we're pushing the play element within our designs. When we first started Buttercrumble, we knew we'd always make sure it was exciting. It's important to keep your joie de vivre and embrace a little merrymaking. We're here for the kindred spirits who embrace openness and interaction through activities such as co-design.

When all's said and done, with a name like Buttercrumble, we just have to have fun with design! After all, what the world really needs is a return to joy and sweetness. To discover more of our world, please visit: www.buttercrumble.com.

# ACKNOWLEDGMENTS

Creativity is innate. However, its seemingly effortless and magical quality is – as we say – "seemingly". We are grateful to the cheerleaders who recognise the hard work, determination, and patience required to pursue a creative career or entrepreneurship.

The words in this book would not fulfil their true potential without the support of our publishing team at BIS. Thank you for sharing the light. You've been the North Star on our journey, and we'll pass our light forward.

Our design partners have privileged us to be creative every day and the real joy happens when creativity is shared; it comes from the heart, mind, and soul of the maker. They enable us to work together on global projects that make a difference.

Thanks to our close friends, Jessica Grady and Gareth Dakin, who have supported us and are mentioned in our book. These are those who understand the unique challenges of running a creative business, and we would not be without their straight-talking nature.

Our most steadfast entrepreneurial community belongs to the University of Leeds. There have been many key guides along the way, including our tutors within the School of Design and the Spark Team. Without them, we wouldn't have considered transforming our hobby into a business. Thank you to fellow alumni, the talented Lucy Jones who captured the cover photography in our early days and to the inspiring Sarah Oglesby who captured the portrait within the book.

Finally, we are grateful to our humble family. Our parents and grandparents may as well be non-executive directors on "the board". They have tolerated numerous twin pranks, spats, and quirks. This is especially true for our husbands and for Emily who each deserve a medal for their sense of humour.

The list could be endless, as we have met so many luminaries on our journey. This is for everyone who has supported us – thank you!

# REFERENCES

The following publications and websites were referenced whilst writing this book:

Aaker, D. 2010. *Building Strong Brands*. 9th ed. London: Simon & Schuster

Borden, N.H., 1964. The concept of the marketing mix. *Journal of Advertising Research*, 4(2), pp.2-7.

Bloomberg. 2018. *Tiffany & Co. Has Built a Secret Lab to Crush Its Rivals*. [Online]. [Date accessed: 3rd April 2022]. Available from: https://www.bloomberg.com/news/articles/2018-07-18/tiffany-amp-co-has-built-a-secret-lab-of-shiny-dreams

Bouhali, R., Mekdad, Y., Lebsir, H. and Ferkha, L., 2015. Leader roles for innovation: Strategic thinking and planning. *Procedia-Social and Behavioral Sciences*, 181, pp.72-78.

Business Centre. 2018. *Embrace the Naive Expert*. [Online]. [Date accessed: 25th June 2020]. Available from: https://www.businesscentre.com.au/news/embrace-the-naive-expert

Butter, S. 2020. *The Wing: how the 'feminist utopia' got it so wrong*. Evening Standard. [Online]. 7 July. [Accessed 3 April 2022]. Available from: https://www.standard.co.uk/lifestyle/the-wing-rise-and-fall-a4491126.html

Crow, D. 2003. *Visible Signs*. Crans-près-Céligny: AVA Publishing SA

Dweck, C. 2017. *Mindset — Updated Edition: Changing The Way You Think To Fulfil Your Potential*. 6th Ed. Hachette UK

Edelman, D. C. Branding in the digital age. *Harvard Business Review*, 88(12), pp.62-69.

Google Trends. 2020. *Branding agency — Explore — Google Trends*. [Online]. [Date accessed: 10th June 2020]. Available from: https://trends.google.com/trends/explore

Harper, S. 2020. *How Co-living Communities Will Replace Our Empty Offices.* [Online]. [Date Accessed: 31st May 2021]. Available from: https://www.wired.co.uk/article/co-working-community

*Harvard Business Review*, 2021, Volume 99, Issue 3, Women are Better Leaders—Especially in a Crisis. P.30

Heathcote, E. 2020. *The curse of the Airbnb aesthetic.* Financial Times. [Online]. 21 August. [Date accessed: 31st August 2020]. Available from: https://on.ft.com/2QaboKc

Hunt, V. Et al. 2020. *Diversity wins: How inclusion matters.* [Online]. McKinsey & Company. [Accessed 8 April 2021]. Available from: https://www.mckinsey.com/featured-insights/diversity-and-inclusion/diversity-wins-how-inclusion-matters

Leader Lab. 2010. *Connie Kalcher on LEGO Mindstorms, LEGO Design By Me and LEGO Universe.* [Online]. [Date accessed: 28 July 2020]. Available from: https://www.youtube.com/watch?v=Ml51gH5KUns

Lexico Powered by Oxford. 2019. *s.v. Principle.* [Online]. [Date accessed: 21st April 2020]. Available from: https://www.lexico.com/definition/principle

McKinsey & Company. 2010. *The five attributes of enduring family businesses.* [Online]. [Accessed 1 November 2022]. Available from: https://www.mckinsey.com/capabilities/people-and-organizational-performance/our-insights/the-five-attributes-of-enduring-family-businesses

Pahud de Mortanges, C. and Van Riel, A. 2003. Brand Equity and Shareholder Value. *European Management Journal.* 21, pp. 521-527.

Portas, M. 2018. *Work Like a Woman. A Manifesto for Change.* London: Bantam Press. Acessed: 28 April 2020]. Available from: https://youtu.be/Ml51gH5KUns

Sawhney, M, Wolcott, R and Arroniz, I. 2007. The Twelve Different Ways for Companies to Innovate. *Engineering Management Review.* 35(1), 45.

Steare, R. 2020. *Safety at work goes beyond pandemic worries*. Financial Times. [Online]. 27 July. [Date accessed: 28 July 2020]. Available from: https://www.ft.com/content/af37c3f8-32f0-4574-b86b-143ce021ef38

Short, J.R., 1989. Yuppies, yuffies and the new urban order. *Transactions of the Institute of British Geographers*, pp.173-188.

The Coca-Cola Company. 2020. *Purpose & Company Vision*. [Online]. [Date accessed: 15 April 2020]. Available from: https://www.coca-colacompany.com/company/purpose-and-vision

Toms. 2020. *Your Impact*. [Online]. [Date accessed: 15 April 2020]. Available from: https://www.toms.com/impact

WGSN. 2020. *Executive Summary Future Consumer 2022*. [Online]. [Date accessed: 29 April 2020]. Available from: https://www.wgsn.com/en/

WGSN. 2021. *Consumer Lifestyles 2023*. [Online]. [Date Accessed: 31st May 2021]. Available from: https://www.wgsn.com/en